ANALYSIS
FOR
MARKETING PLANNING

ANALYSIS
FOR
MARKETING PLANNING

Donald R. Lehmann

Graduate School of Business
Columbia University

Russell S. Winer

Owen Graduate School of Management
Vanderbilt University

1988

BPI
IRWIN

Homewood, Illinois 60430

Editor: John R. Weimeister
Developmental editor: Rhonda K. Harris
Production editor: Ann Cassady
Copyediting coordinator: Jean Roberts
Production manager: Bette Ittersagen
Cover calligrapher: John Thoeming
Artist: D. Gaeta
Compositor: Western Interface
Typeface: 11/13 Times Roman
Printer: Arcata/Kingsport

ISBN 0-256-05783-4
Library of Congress Catalog Card No. 87–61994

Printed in the United States of America

2 3 4 5 6 7 8 9 0 K 5 4 3 2 1 0 9

To Kris, Bart, and Kelly
and
To Toby, Jessica, and Andrew

PREFACE

RATIONALE

This book evolved from a course given at the Columbia Business School called Marketing Planning and Strategy. In the mid-1970s, the marketing faculty at Columbia realized that traditional marketing management courses in business school curricula were fine for preparing MBA students for senior-level marketing positions, but did not equip them with the tools necessary for first jobs with such titles as "assistant brand manager" or "assistant account executive." This is because the basic content of marketing management courses is oriented toward the development of marketing strategy which is often the responsibility of the bosses of the newly minted MBAs. It was felt that students needed a more "hands-on" course which would prepare them for the data collection and analysis tasks that often fall to junior-level managers.

The hands-on, practical course that is now required for marketing majors at Columbia and that is being increasingly offered as an elective at other leading business schools is based on the operating, usually annual, marketing plan. The exercise of actually developing a marketing plan is highly integrative as it brings together concepts learned from marketing research, marketing strategy, finance, production, and corporate policy courses.

This book does not attempt to cover all aspects of the marketing plan. However, we focus on what we feel are the activities most relevant to junior-level managers, that is, the analysis of information pertaining to a product's environment, customers, and competitors. In addition, Chapter 1 contains a complete overview of an operating marketing plan. As such, the book can be used as a stand-alone text in conjunction with case studies, or it can be used as a companion text to books on strategic marketing management, which tend to focus more on what to do after the type of analysis treated in this book has been completed.

OUTLINE OF THE BOOK

The book has six major chapters:

1. Overview of Marketing Planning.   In this chapter, we present

the rationale for planning, pitfalls that should be avoided, and an outline of a complete marketing plan.

2. Defining Competition. One of the most challenging decisions faced by marketing managers is that of defining the competition since the set of competitors can usually be constructed as narrowly or as broadly as desired. This chapter discusses methods for defining competition on different levels of generality.

3. Analyzing Industry Attractiveness. Fundamental criteria for evaluating a product's position in the market are aggregate factors such as market growth rate, industry factors such as barriers to entry, and environmental factors such as regulation.

4. Competitor Analysis. Monitoring competitors' strategies and anticipating their future moves is a key to the development of successful marketing strategy. This chapter covers how to analyze competition in terms of competitors' objectives, strategies, and capabilities, and predicting future actions.

5. Customer Analysis. At the core of modern thinking about marketing is a customer orientation. In this chapter, we discuss the key information required to monitor customer behavior.

6. Market Potential and Forecasting. In this chapter, we describe methods for estimating the potential size of a market and predicting future levels of sales and/or market share.

The book provides discussion of specific analytical methods and data sources which can be useful for each of the analyses discussed in the chapters as well as some useful formats for summarizing the information.

ACKNOWLEDGMENTS

We would like to acknowledge our former students at Columbia and Vanderbilt universities, who have stimulated our thoughts and given us incentive to improve our understanding of marketing planning. We have received valuable comments from the reviewers and colleagues at our current schools and other universities. This latter group includes particularly: Mac Hulbert and Joel Steckel at Columbia; Allan Shocker of the University of Washington; Kim Corfman of New York University; and Sharon E. Beatty, University of Alabama. We also thank Kris Lehmann for her help.

Donald R. Lehmann
Russell S. Winer

CONTENTS

Sep 8

Sep 16

ix

CHAPTER 1

MARKETING PLANNING

OVERVIEW

Definition and Objectives of Plans

Marketing planning has become a major activity in most firms. A recent survey (Hulbert, Lehmann, & Hoenig, 1987) found that over 90 percent of marketing executives were engaged in formal planning. The executives, on average, spend 45 days a year involved in planning, and they rely most heavily on information from the sales force, management information systems, and internal marketing research. The developmental plans, which are generally annual in nature and focus on product/product line or market, are thus an important function for marketers, one that is seen as beneficial for improving both coordination and performance.

The marketing plan can be divided into two general parts: the situation analysis which analyzes the market, and the objectives, strategy, and programs which direct the firm's actions. While most books and the popular press concentrate on the latter, it can be concluded that incorrect or inadequate analysis will often lead to poor decisions regarding actions. Therefore, this book is devoted to the mundane but critical task of providing the analysis on which to base an action plan—in short, the marketing homework.

More specifically, the purpose of this book is to provide its readers with guidelines for preparing the central parts of the background analysis necessary to develop a marketing plan, customer, competitor, and industry analysis, plus planning assumptions and forecasting. Since we do not aim to discuss every element involved in marketing planning, the topics covered will be discussed using a strong practitioner orientation, in other words, a "how-to" perspective.

What is a **marketing plan**? A working definition might be:

1

A marketing plan is a *written* document containing the guidelines for the *business center's* marketing programs and allocations over the *planning period*.

Several parts of the above definition have been emphasized and merit further explanation.

First, note that the plan is a written document, not something stored in a manager's head. This characteristic of marketing plans produces multiple benefits. Also it encourages and requires disciplined thinking. It ensures that prior experiences in terms of strategies that succeeded or failed are not lost. It provides a vehicle for communications between functional areas of the firm, such as manufacturing, finance, and sales, which is so vital to the successful implementation of a plan. The marketing plan also facilitates the pinpointing of responsibility for achieving results by a specified date. Finally, a written plan provides for continuity when there is management turnover and for quickly indoctrinating new employees to the situation facing the business.

A second aspect of the marketing plan definition to note is that it is usually written at the business center level. This is purposely vague since the precise level at which plans are written varies from organization to organization. For example, in a typical brand management–organized company, a marketing plan is written for each brand since it is a profit center. Alternatively, some companies write plans for groups of brands or services, particularly when direct fixed costs are difficult to allocate by individual product. Thus, while marketing planning activities commonly exist, it is difficult to provide a general statement of the organizational level at which they operate.

For example, General Foods develops a separate marketing plan for each brand of cereal marketed by the Post Division, such as Raisin Bran and Grape Nuts. Alternatively, McDonald's has one overall marketing plan for its fast-food operations, with perhaps some regional differences, because it does not make sense to develop isolated plans for Chicken McNuggets and the McDLT sandwich.

A final item to note from the definition of a marketing plan is that the planning period or horizon varies from product to product. Retailing traditionally has short planning cycles to match the seasonality and vagaries of fashion trends. Automobiles, however, have longer planning cycles since lead times to product development and/or modifications are longer. Other factors contributing to variation in the length of planning horizons are rates of technological change, intensity of competition, and frequency of shifts in the tastes of relevant groups of customers. The typical horizon, however, is annual. This is supported by data reported in Table 1–1.

In summary, the marketing plan is an operational document. While it contains strategies for the business center, it is more short-term oriented than what might be called a strategic plan. Strategic plans are usually of longer duration (three to five years), more general in describing business center strategies, and of a more aggregate, higher-level nature. Marketing plans are specific statements of how to achieve short-term results.

In fact, the objectives of a marketing plan can be stated concisely as to:

1. Define the current business situation (and how we got there).
2. Define problems and opportunities facing the business.
3. Establish objectives.
4. Define the strategies and programs necessary to achieve the objectives.
5. Pinpoint responsibility for business center objectives.
6. Establish timetables for achieving objectives.
7. Encourage careful and disciplined thinking.
8. Establish a customer/competitor orientation.

This last marketing plan objective is particularly relevant for this book. Most managers are aware of the marketing concept popularized in

TABLE 1–1
Time Horizons for Marketing Plans

Time Period	Industrial Products	Consumer Products	Service Firms
Less than one year	1%	6%	— %
One year	18	23	14
One year, plus brief reference to later years	44	40	58
One year, plus a separate longer-range plan	18	16	—
More than one year	19	15	28
	100%	100%	100%

Source: David S. Hopkins, *The Marketing Plan* (New York: The Conference Board, 1981), p. 10. © 1981 The Conference Board.

the 1960s which dictates that markets must maintain a customer orientation in all their strategies. Less commonly acknowledged is the fact that a competitor orientation, especially in today's business environment, is as important. The vast majority of products and services do not enjoy monopolies; competitors often determine a brand's profits as much as any action taken by the marketing manager. By emphasizing the importance of having both a customer and competitor orientation, we believe we are focusing this book on the two most important components of the strategy development process.

Frequent Mistakes in the Planning Process

Unfortunately, not all organizations attempting to develop marketing plans have been pleased with the process. The Strategic Planning Institute has identified the most common mistakes in strategy planning which seem relevant to marketing planning as well.

The Speed of the Process
This is the problem of either being so slow that the process seems to go on continuously or so fast that there is an extreme burst of activity to rush out of a plan. In the former case, managers become "burned out" by constantly filling out forms which can distract them from operational tasks. In the latter case, such a quickie can easily lead to critical oversights that affect the strategies developed.

The Amount of Data Collected
It is important to collect sufficient data to properly estimate customer needs and competitive trends. However, as in many other situations, the economic law of diminishing returns quickly sets in on the data collection process. It is usually the case that a small percentage of all the data available produces a large percentage of the insights obtainable. We hope this book will be useful in describing the data considered most essential.

Who Does the Planning
In the late 1960s, strategic planning models developed by the Boston Consulting Group, McKinsey, General Electric, and others led to the formation of formal strategic planning groups in many major corporations. Essentially, the planning process was delegated to the professional planners, while implementation of the plans was left to the line managers. Naturally, line managers felt resentment against such a process as

they thought that the planners had no "feel" for the markets for which they were planning; that is, it was managing totally by the numbers rather than including any market intuition gleaned from experience. As a result, hostility grew between the staff planners and line managers to the point where recommended strategies were either poorly implemented or ignored. At the present time, due to both poor results from staff-directed planning efforts and the recession of 1982–83 which led to large cuts in corporate staffs, line managers are much more involved with planning, both strategic and marketing (*Business Week,* 1984). The conclusion seems to be that line managers should indeed develop marketing plans but with staff assistance.

The Structure
Clearly, any formal planning effort involves some structure. The advantage of structure is that it forces discipline on the planners; that is, certain data must be collected. Interestingly, many firms believe that the most important result of planning is not the plan itself but merely the necessity of structuring thought about the strategic issues facing the business. However, an apparent danger is that the structure can take precedence over the content so that planning becomes mere form-filling or number crunching with little thought to the purposes of the effort. Thus, while the process should not be too bureaucratic, there must be enough structure to force completion. A good solution to the dilemma is to consider the plan format as a guide but with a rigid timetable. Flexibility in format helps to prevent the plan from being mindless paper shuffling.

Length of Plan
The length of a marketing plan must be balanced between being too long so that it is ignored by both line and senior managers and being too brief so that it ignores key details. Many organizations have formal guidelines for the optimal lengths of documents (e.g., Procter & Gamble's dreaded one-page limit on memos) so that what is long for one firm is optimal for another. A modal length, however, is about 20 to 50 pages.

How Often Planning Is Done
The decision concerning the length of the planning cycle was discussed earlier. A common mistake made in planning is to plan either more frequently or less frequently than necessary. In the former case, the frequent reevaluation of strategies can lead to erratic firm behavior. Also,

the planning process is more burdensome than it needs to be. For instance, where plans are not revised frequently, the business may not adapt quickly enough to changes in the environment and thus suffer a deterioration in its competitive position. Actually, environmental conditions such as tax returns and reporting requirements tend to favor an annual plan.

Number of Alternative Strategies Considered

The problems encountered of this type are either too few alternatives discussed, thus raising the likelihood of failure, or too many, which increases the time and cost of the planning effort. Multiple alternatives should be considered, but this does not necessarily imply that everyone needs to be heard. It is important to have diversity in the strategic options (e.g., both growth and hold strategies) since discarded strategies often prove to be useful as contingency plans.

Who Sees the Plan?

For the successful implementation of a marketing plan, a broad consensus including other functional areas is required. For example, a high-quality strategy is difficult to implement if manufacturing is not simultaneously exerting high-quality control. On the other hand, growth objectives may be achievable only through the relaxation of credit policies. A common mistake is to view the plan as a proprietary possession of marketing management.

Not Using the Plan as a Sales Document

A major but often overlooked purpose of a plan and its presentation is to generate funds from either internal sources (i.e., to gain budget approval) or external sources (i.e., to gain a partner for a joint venture). To state it differently, the plan and its proponents compete with other plans and their proponents for scarce resources. Therefore, the more appealing the plan and the better the track record of its proponents, the better the chance of budget approval.

THE PLANNING PROCESS

Approaches to Planning

Two general approaches to planning have developed. "Top-down" planning refers to a process where the marketing plans are formulated either by senior or middle management with the aid of staff, and the plans are implemented by lower-echelon personnel such as sales representatives. An alternative to such top-down approaches are "bottom-up" methods where the lower ranks are actively involved with the planning process in terms of forecasts and the collection of competitor and customer information. Such information is subject to higher-level review, but in such a planning system, the lower management personnel play a key role in the process.

Both systems have some commendable characteristics. The rationale often used for top-down planning is that the higher the level the person occupies in the organization, the better the perspective that person has of the context of the problems facing the business. Field salespeople, for example, tend to consider the competitive battleground as their sales territory and not necessarily the national or even international market. Bottom-up planning systems are often characterized by better implementation than top-down approaches since the people primarily charged with executing the plan are involved with developing it.

Steps in the Planning Process

In most organizations, the necessity to collect information and the structure of the marketing plan impose a need to have a programmed sequence of events occur in the planning process. These events generally follow the order of Steps 1–8 below and as shown in Figure 1–1.

Step 1. Updating Facts about the Past. Data collected for marketing planning purposes are often either provisional or estimated. For example, in planning for 1989, actual market size data for 1988 may not be available because of delays in the aggregate data collection process. However, forecasts for 1988 developed in 1987 are often available. Alternatively, preliminary estimates of the gross national product for 1988 may exist but not the final figures.

Step 2. Collecting Background Data. The data collection effort focuses on information available on the current situation. This is, appropriately, termed the situation analysis that will be described later.

Step 3. Analyzing Historical and Background Data. Existing data are analyzed in order to forecast competitors' actions, customers' behavior, economic conditions, and so forth. Such an analysis need not be quantitative; in fact, much of the analysis, as will be seen in later chap-

FIGURE 1–1
Marketing Planning Sequence

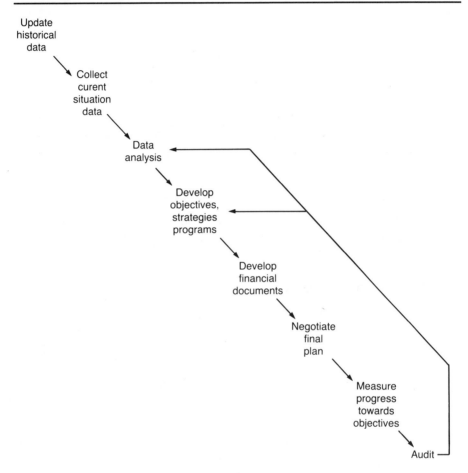

ters, is qualitative with the emphasis being on drawing implications from nonnumerical data. This analysis leads to the delineation of key opportunities and threats to the business.

Step 4. Developing Objectives, Strategies, Action Programs. The implications drawn from the background data (see Step 3) are used to formulate brand objectives, strategies, and marketing mix decisions. This is, in fact, the critical activity of the planning process because it outlines in detail what will be done with the brand during the year (or appropriate planning period). However, the order of the steps indicates that logical strategic thinking cannot be done without considering the facts at hand.

The objectives, strategies, and mix decisions are constrained by company mission, objectives and strategy, company policy and resources, and legal considerations, among others. Thus, this part of the process generally involves (*a*) setting objectives, (*b*) developing strategies and programs to achieve the objectives, (*c*) comparing the programs in terms of their ability to achieve objectives (e.g., profit) *and* to be acceptable in terms of company policy and legal constraints, and (*d*) selecting a basic objective, strategy, and program combination.

Step 5. Developing Pro Forma Financial Statements.   Such statements typically include budgets and profit and loss (income) figures.

Step 6. Negotiating.   Rarely, if ever, is the market plan generated from Steps 1 to 5 implemented without several rounds of negotiations with senior management. In a brand management organizational structure, the plans themselves must be marketed as managers vie for their desired portions of corporate resources. In large organizations, this negotiation phase can last as long as all the prior steps.

Step 7. Measuring Progress.   In order to make necessary corrections to the plan as the environment changes within the planning period, the progress of the plan toward the stated objectives must be monitored. This implies that marketing research and other information relevant to measuring the quantities stated as objectives (e.g., market share and sales) must be collected on an interim basis.

Step 8. Auditing.   After a planning period, it is customary to go back over the period and determine variances of planned versus actual results and sources of the variances. This audit provides important diagnostic information for both current and future planning efforts and thus acts as a source of feedback to the planning effort.

The planning sequence is therefore a logical flow of events leading from data collection and analysis to strategy formulation to auditing the performance of the plan. It implies that sound strategic thinking cannot occur until the planner has sufficiently utilized available information from which implications can be drawn about future market conditions.

COMPONENTS OF THE MARKETING PLAN

While nearly every firm utilizing marketing plans has its own format (see Hopkins, 1981, for examples), a common set of elements can be enumerated. A sample of a complete marketing plan outline is provided as an appendix to this chapter and is summarized in Figure 1–2. This outline describes the major areas of analysis and data collection required for a "typical" marketing plan. The rationale and a brief description of the contents of each major component of the plan are provided to give the reader an overview of the plan and the context in which this book is set.

The Executive Summary

A senior manager is often in a position where he or she has to review many marketing plans. In such situations, a brief summary of the marketing plan focusing on the objectives, strategies, and expected financial performance is mandatory.

Background Assessment

The data and concomitant analysis so vital to developing sound marketing strategies can be split into two parts. First, the historical appraisal seeks to identify long-term trends and short-term changes in the market. This section applies to past data; that is, if we are planning for 1989 in 1988, historical data will include 1987 and older information. Some of

FIGURE 1–2
Marketing Plan Summary

    I.   Executive summary.
   II.   Background assessment:
       A.   Historical appraisal.
       B.   Situation analysis.
       C.   Planning assumptions.
  III.   Marketing objectives.
  IV.   Marketing strategy.
   V.   Marketing programs.
  VI.   Financial documents.
 VII.   Monitors and controls.
VIII.   Contingency plans.

---

the major areas of interest here are general market data, such as sales and market shares; market activity information, such as advertising and pricing histories; historical cost and profit data; and facts related to changes in technology, regulations, or other general environmental conditions. Since this data becomes voluminous over time, it is often stored in a separate document called a Product Fact Book.

The situation analysis is the second major component of the background analysis. This is a detailed study of current events and is composed of several parts, discussed below.

1. Sales Analysis.   This is an intensive study of a brand's sales records intended to uncover problems that are hidden by aggregate numbers. For example, an overall sales increase of a line of shoes may be hiding the fact that the sales of a particular size or color are dropping.

2. Industry Attractiveness Analysis.   Since all markets are dynamic in that competitors, customers, technology, and sales growth rates change, the underlying attractiveness of an industry as a target for investment also changes. The purpose of this section of the marketing plan is to identify those factors which can be used to assess the attractiveness of an industry in which the firm is competing at a given point in time.

3. Customer Analysis.   This section of the situation analysis is an attempt to guarantee the customer orientation that is critical to the success of the product. It is vital to understand not only who the customers are but also how and why they behave as they do.

4. Competitor Analysis.   What are the key competitors in the market likely to do in the future? That is the key question addressed by this section of the plan. Since virtually all markets are competitive, it is easy to see why this is a vital section.

5. Resource Analysis.   This optional section of the plan is a competitor analysis of the brand for which the plan is being written. In other words, strengths and weaknesses of the brand of interest are determined by comparison to the major competitors.

The third part of the background assessment deals with planning assumptions. Such assumptions involve a wide variety of quantities. First, market potential for the product is a key number since it has implications for expected future category growth, resource allocation, and many other constructs related to decision making. Market and brand forecasts are relevant for this section as well. Finally, assumptions made about exogenous factors, such as raw materials or labor supply, are relevant.

The background assessment forms the "homework" part of the plan necessary before marketing objectives and strategies can be formulated. While it is perhaps more enjoyable to develop concepts of where a business should go during the next planning horizon, the up-front data collection and analysis are the most vital part of the plan since time spent drawing implications from the background data often makes the optimal strategies relatively apparent.

The Marketing Strategy Section

It is logical that the background assessment be followed by the strategy portion of the plan. This part is actually comprised of three sections: a statement of marketing objectives ("Where do we want to go?"), the marketing strategy itself ("Generally, how are we going to get there?"), and the marketing programs consisting of the marketing mix elements ("Exactly what do we do in what order?").

The Rest of the Plan

The final three parts of the marketing plan do not form a cohesive unit but are vital components. The financial documents report the budgets and pro forma profit and loss (income) statements. Senior managers, naturally, inspect the expected financial outcome with extreme care. In fact, the P&L statements are often the key "sales document" in securing approval for the plan. The monitors and controls section specifies the type of marketing research and other information necessary to measure the progress toward achieving the stated objectives. Thus, the kind of information usually collected is dependent on the objectives; for example, if a market share increase is the objective, then such information must be collected in a timely manner to check for possible shortfalls. Finally, contingency plans are helpful, particularly in dynamic markets where either new products or competitors often create the need for changes in strategy before the end of the plan's horizon. Often, these contingencies are strategies which were previously considered but discarded for some reason.

SUMMARY

The marketing plan can thus be seen as a cohesive document intended to act as a guideline for the allocation of resources for a product. We feel that while there are many good references for the development of strategy, relatively few sources exist for a description of the background analysis necessary to develop prior to strategy formulation. As a result, this book emphasizes the homework part of marketing planning activities.

We aim to be as complete as possible with each topic in that a how-to orientation is taken. In other words, we will discuss the steps necessary to conduct the analyses, provide illustrations of the approaches taken, and, importantly, describe the sources of information typically utilized to perform the analyses. In doing so, we often use examples from consumer packaged goods. This does not indicate we believe the material applies primarily to consumer goods; we believe it applies as well to industrial goods and services. Our choice of examples is dictated by the desire to be understandable to most readers; hence food or clothing serves our pedagogical purposes better than oil well drilling equipment or financial hedging investments.

The basic outline of the book is as follows. Since much of the situation analysis presumes a definition of the industry in which a product is competing, we begin by describing methods employed for defining the competitive set. Once that has been established, Chapter 3 outlines an industry attractiveness analysis. Chapter 4 describes in detail how competitors can be analyzed with an eye toward predicting their likely future strategies. In Chapter 5, we describe approaches for analyzing customers, including methods for identifying market segments. The role of planning assumptions, market potential, and forecasting are detailed in Chapter 6, while in the concluding chapter, we describe a method for putting together all the data and the future of planning with respect to new information collection and analysis technologies.

APPENDIX MARKETING PLAN OUTLINE

I. *Executive Summary.* A one- to three-page synopsis of the plan providing highlights of current situation, objectives, strategies, principal action programs, and financial expectations.

II. *Background Assessment.*

    A. Historical appraisal. Items to consider:

        1. Market.

            a. Size, scope, and share of the market sales history of all producers and their market shares.

            b. Market potential and major trends in supply and demand of this and related products.

        2. Market activity.

            a. Pricing history through all levels of distribution and reasons for principal fluctuations.

            b. The distribution channels.

            c. Selling policies and practices.

            d. Advertising and promotion.

        3. Sales, costs, and gross profits on our product.

            a. Sales history by grades, varieties; by sales district; by end use; by industry.

            b. Cost history.

            c. Profit history.

            d. Changes in volume and profit rankings of product lines and items in a product line.

        4. Technology—Product and process improvements.

            a. Rate (life cycle).

            b. Lead time required for design and development of a new product.

            c. Market impact (primary versus selective demand).

            d. How interrelated are product and process?

        5. Market characteristics: Trends in.

            a. Industry use patterns.

            b. End-use patterns.

            c. Frequency, quantity, and timing of purchase.

            d. Buying procedures and practices.

            e. Service.

        6. Government and social.

            a. Regulatory climate.

            b. Fiscal and monetary policy.

            c. Consumerism.

            d. Environmental impact.

    B. Where to store the information.

        1. The Product Fact Book is a separate but related part of the overall marketing plan comprising the *statistical and permanent record of product and market results,* activities, conditions, and characteristics.

2. Its purpose is to:
  a. Provide a ready reference for all necessary information that forms the basis of the marketing plan.
  b. Permit the basic part of the marketing plan to be relatively brief in form and operational in usage.
  c. Provide a fast and easy way for new personnel to become acquainted with the product and market. (This is especially pertinent, in view of management policy fostering transfers.)
3. Primary responsibility for preparation and maintenance of the Product Fact Book is usually assumed by the senior marketing manager for a product/product line. In most cases, maintenance of a single copy of the Product Fact Book is sufficient.
C. Situation analysis.
  1. Sales analysis: Evaluate performance.
    a. Market area performance versus company average.
    b. Trends of sales, costs, and profits by product lines.
    c. Performance of distributors, end-users, key customers on an index basis.
    d. Past versus current results by area, product, channel, and so on.
    e. Try to use data at a disaggregate level.
  2. Industry attractiveness analysis—Evaluate:
    a. Market factors:
      (1) Size.
      (2) Growth.
      (3) Cyclicality.
      (4) Seasonality.
    b. Industry factors:
      (1) Capacity.
      (2) New product entry prospects.
      (3) Rivalry.
      (4) Power of suppliers.
      (5) Power of buyers.
      (6) Threat of substitutes.
    c. Environmental factors:
      (1) Social.
      (2) Political.
      (3) Demographic.
      (4) Technological.
      (5) Regulatory.
  3. Customer analysis—key questions to better understand your market:

a. Who:

   (1) Who are your customers?

   (2) How can they be classified?

   (3) Which classification is most important to you and your competitors—today and tomorrow?

b. Why:

   (1) Why do customers buy when, as much as, and the way they do?

   (2) How involved and prolonged is the purchase decision?

   (3) How many people are involved and at what level?

   (4) What are the objectives of each person involved?

   (5) Which objectives are most important?

c. What if . . .

   (1) What could cause a change in customers' objectives?

   (2) What information will help anticipate these changes?

d. So what?

   (1) What are the implications of changes in customer behavior?

   (2) What is the expected impact on you and your competitors?

e. What then?

   (1) How will this customer analysis improve your understanding of the total market, size, mix growth rate, and timing?

4. Competitor analysis.

  a. For each major competitor, ask:

   (1) How does he measure and evaluate his results?

   (2) How did he achieve the results and what factors helped or hurt him along the way?

   (3) What are his important strengths and liabilities and how are these likely to change?

   (4) What is his future strategy likely to be?

  b. Thorough analysis requires:

   (1) Exploration of past results.

   (2) Reconstruction of past strategy.

   (3) Evaluation of resources.

     (i) Ability to conceive and design new products.

     (ii) Ability to produce or manufacture.

     (iii) Ability to market.

     (iv) Ability to finance.

     (v) Ability to manage.

        5. Resource analysis.
           a. Evaluate yourself in three contexts:
              (1) Compare your resources with those of others aiming at the same target.
              (2) Weigh them against the requirements of the opportunity or threat you are planning to pursue.
              (3) Assess them in light of the strategic questions already raised by the customer and competitor analysis.
           b. What to evaluate.
              (1) Ability to conceive and design.
              (2) Ability to produce.
              (3) Ability to market.
              (4) Ability to finance.
              (5) Ability to manage.
              (6) Will to succeed in this business.
    D. Planning assumptions.
        1. Explicit strategy of assumptions about future.
        2. Projections, predictions and forecasts.
III. *Marketing Objectives.*
    A. Corporate objectives (if appropriate).
    B. Divisional objectives (if appropriate).
    C. Marketing objectives.
        1. Quantity (sales, share, and so on).
        2. Direction.
        3. Number.
        4. Time frame.
        5. Rationale.
IV. *Marketing Strategy.* How the objectives will be achieved. Elements:
    A. Strategic alternative(s).
    B. Customer targets.
    C. Competitor targets.
    D. Core strategy.
 V. *Marketing Programs.*
    A. Pricing.
    B. Advertising/promotion.
        1. Copy.
        2. Media.
        3. Trade versus consumer promotion.
    C. Sales/distribution.
    D. Product development.
    E. Market research.

    Note: Sections of IV and V are often combined to reduce redundancy and to make the plan easier to read.

VI. *Financial Documents.*
   A. Budgets.
      1. Advertising/promotion.
      2. Sales.
      3. Research.
      4. Product development.
   B. Pro forma statements.
      1. Costs.
         a. Dollar, unit.
         b. Variable, fixed.
      2. Revenues (forecasted).
      3. Profits.
         a. Dollars, dollars per unit.
         b. ROI.
         c. Versus company average.
VII. *Monitors and Controls.* Specific research information to be used:
   A. Secondary data.
      1. Sales reports.
      2. Orders.
      3. Informal sources.
   B. Primary data.
      1. Store audits (Nielsen, SAMI).
      2. Specialized consulting firms.
      3. Consumer panel.
VIII. *Contingency Plans and Other Miscellaneous Documents.*
   A. Contingency plans.
   B. Alternative strategies considered.
   C. Miscellaneous.

REFERENCES

Hopkins, David. *The Marketing Plan.* New York: The Conference Board, 1981.

Hulbert, James M.; Donald R. Lehmann; and Scott Hoenig. "Practices and Impacts of Marketing Planning." Working Paper, Graduate School of Business, Columbia University, 1987.

"The New Breed of Strategic Planner." *Business Week,* September 17, 1984, p. 62.

CHAPTER 2

DEFINING THE COMPETITIVE SET

OVERVIEW

Consider the following quote from *Advertising Age* attributed to a copywriter at Ted Bates:

> A Bates writer can't write until someone points out the enemy.... If your share goes up, somebody else's share must go down. I want to know that somebody else.... Many categories have stopped growing so it's more important than ever to know where you're going to get your customers.

The purpose of this chapter is to help marketing managers determine the identity of the "enemy." A distinct precondition to both analyzing competitors' capabilities and developing competitive strategy is the assessment of the sources of competitive threat.

In some sense, everything competes with everything else. The key question, therefore, is not whether products or services compete but the extent to which they compete. Defining competition therefore requires a balance between identifying too many competitors (and therefore complicating instead of simplifying decision making) and identifying too few (and overlooking a key set).

Although it is typically felt that the competitive arena involves the fight for customers, such as sales, there are other bases on which competitors tangle. For example, IBM and Emerson Electric, noncompetitors in terms of customers, compete for electrical engineers, for instance, the same labor supply. Kodak and jewelers compete for silver, that is, raw materials. Avon and Tupperware compete for home demonstration sales: the same channel of distribution. Similarly, all manufacturers who sell through supermarkets and department stores compete for shelf space. Geographically based competition is important for many firms such as local retailers; for example, hardware stores, and multinational firms, such as Ericsson (Sweden), NEC (Japan), and Northern Telecom (Canada), in the market for telecommunications equipment. In other words, competition exists in many dimensions. Therefore, it is important to consider all types of competition as listed in Table 2–1.

As Table 2–1 suggests, competition can be based on many factors and is not necessarily even intentional. For example, the battle for shelf facings in supermarkets has led to a variety of manufacturer concessions to retailers to obtain desirable shelf positions, and the struggle for shelf space occurs across as well as within traditional product category boundaries.

Perhaps the most crucial competition occurs *within* a company, when different units in an organization ask for funds. In this competition, the plan acts mainly as a sales document, and its financial projections often become the key to the sale. This competition is often intentional as it puts pressure on product managers to develop sound marketing plans.

Misdefinition of the competitive set can have a serious impact on the success of a marketing plan, especially in the long run. One problem is that an important competitive threat can be overlooked. For example, the Swiss had the market for premium watches and Timex the market for inexpensive watches to themselves for many years. When the Japanese firms developed electronic watches in the 1970s, they were not viewed as a threat to either business because the Japanese were not viewed as

TABLE 2–1
Bases on Which Competition Exists

   I. Customer-oriented:
      Who they are: Competition for same budget.
      When they use it.
      Why they used it: Benefits sought.
  II. Marketing-oriented: Advertising and promotion:
      Theme/copy strategy.
      Media.
      Distribution.
      Price.
 III. Resource-oriented:
      Raw materials.
      Employees.
      Financial resources.
 IV. Geographic

serious competition. History, of course, tells a different story; Timex was forced to develop electronic watches, while the Swiss added lines using electronic works.

Similarly, steelmakers are only now reacting to the intrusion of plastics into the automobile market. Such an acknowledgment years ago would have produced new products with the lighter-weight advantage of plastics and, perhaps, helped to prevent or at least to slow down the industry's recent dramatic decline.

Moreover, an uncertain definition of the competition creates uncertainty in market definition and, therefore, market-related statistics such as market share. This leaves open the possible manipulation of market boundaries, particularly when compensation or allocation decisions are at stake. For example, assume an objective for Pepsi Light is to gain a 10 percent market share. The ability to achieve this objective depends on whether Pepsi Light competes in the diet soft drink market, the diet cola market, or the caffeine-free market. Thus, deciding in which market you wish to compete is important for both developing and controlling the marketing planning effort.

In this chapter, therefore, we are taking the view that the definition of the competitive set ultimately affects what strategy is pursued. Not all authors subscribe to this approach. Abell (1980), for example, feels that the corporate mission or business definition selected affects the set of competitors against which a firm fights. Unfortunately, competitors usually do not care how a company chooses to define itself and are thus free to compete against a firm's brands even if that firm does not define itself in a way that would include a certain set of brands or companies as competitors.

In this chapter, we present several levels of competition which can be useful for conceptualizing the competitive set. In addition, we discuss methods that can be employed to determine the competition at the various levels. Finally, the notion of enterprise competition, that of firms competing against each other, is described and explained in terms of analyzing competitors.

LEVELS OF MARKET COMPETITION

One way to delineate the set of competitors facing a brand is to consider other products in terms of their proximity to the physical attributes of the brand. Using Figure 2–1 as a guide, the problem of defining competition can be viewed as defining a set of concentric circles with the brand in question at the center.

1. The narrowest perspective one can take of competition is called *product form*. This reflects the view that the main competitors are those brands in the product category which are going after the same segment. For example, two hospitals, each with maternity facilities, might not be thought to be competing if one is appealing to a market segment desiring single rooms and lavish food and surroundings while the other provides semiprivate rooms and standard hospital food. Similarly, although Com-

FIGURE 2–1
Example of Levels of Competition

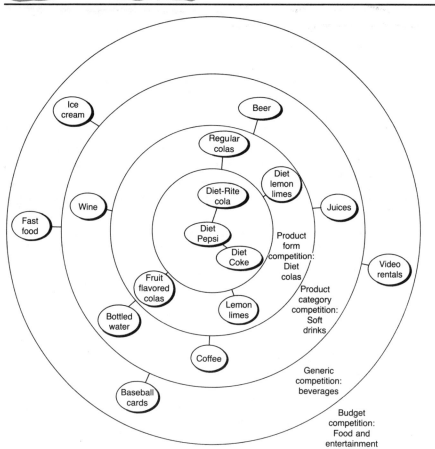

modore, IBM, and Apple all offer personal computers, because of differences in software and available peripheral equipment, only the latter two compete actively for the business market while the former concentrates on home users. Thus, product form competition is a narrow view of competition and focuses mainly on what competitors' current offerings are and not what could happen in the (possibly near) future.

2. The second level of competition is based on those products or services with *similar features,* a feature being defined as the presence of a characteristic (e.g., calories), not its value (e.g., high or low). This type of competition, called *product category,* is what managers naturally think of in terms of a definition for the competitive set. For example, all firms producing linerboard, regardless of the quality, are competitors. All soft drinks form a "market" as well. This is, in fact, the traditional way to determine market composition. Firms specializing in the collection of retail sales data, such as A. C. Nielsen and SAMI, define product categories or markets based on the similarity of physical attributes. While somewhat broader than product form competition, this product category definition of competition still takes a short-run view of the market definition problem.

3. The third level of competition is more long term in nature and focuses on substitutable product categories. Termed *generic competition* by Kotler (1984), it defines the competition and, therefore, the market as consisting of those products or services fulfilling the same customer need. Thus, soft drinks compete with orange juice in the "thirst-quenching" market, fast-food outlets compete against frozen entrées in the "convenience" eating market, and so on.

This need-based perspective is essential if a manager wishes to avoid both overlooking threats and ignoring opportunities. This perspective is well described in Levitt's (1960) classic article which admonishes several industries for defining their businesses too narrowly. Railroads viewed themselves as providing rail-based transportation services and lost much business to trucks and airlines. Steel companies thought they were providing steel rather than general structural material; also, automobile manufacturers wanted the latter so they substituted plastics in some areas of the cars. Some firms take this generic perspective. Federal Express, for example, saw its competitors as not only Purolator, UPS, and the U.S. Postal Service, but also other companies providing quick transmission of information. As a result, they are developing their facsimile business as an alternative to overnight package and small letter delivery.

4. An even more general level of competition which can be consid-

ered is termed *rivalry* by Kotler (1984) and may be better described as
budget competition. This is the broadest view of competition as it considers all products and services competing for the same customer dollar
as forming a market. For example, if a consumer has $500 in discretion-
ary disposable income, he or she could spend it on a vacation, a ring, a
money market instrument, or a variety of other things. A recent article in
The Wall Street Journal (1986) noted that because of the healthy U.S.
economy, people have been spending money on consumer durables rather
than at fast-food chains such as Wendy's or McDonald's. While this view
of competition is conceptually useful, it is very difficult to implement
strategically as it implies an enormous number of competitors.

Some examples should put the market definition issue in perspective. Consider the problem facing the marketing manager for a line of
low-priced stereo components such as Pioneer. What competition does
she/he face? First, there are the competitors fighting for the same segment of the stereo market. Second, there are other, higher-priced component manufacturers. Third, manufacturers of other entertainment products such as TVs and videocassette recorders must be considered. Finally,
alternative ways to spend the money, such as on a vacation, could be
relevant. These different sets of competitors imply multiple marketing
tasks. First, the manager's brand must be shown to have advantages over
competitors' brands in the low-price segment. Second, the advantages of
the low-price components over more expensive (e.g., Bang and Olufsen,
McIntosh) must be established. Third, the customers must be convinced
to buy stereos rather than, say, VCRs. Finally, the prospects have to be
informed about the benefits of buying stereos instead of going on vacation or buying stocks. Thus, market definition has implications not only
for defining the market but for the strategy employed as well.

As a second example, consider the problem facing the product manager for Diet Pepsi. Clearly it competes with other diet colas such as Diet
Coke. Also, it competes with other soft drinks, especially nondiet colas
and diet lemon-limes which differ in only one aspect from diet colas.
Further, it competes with most food and beverages (wines and bottled
waters as a drink with a meal, ice creams as a treat, and so forth).
Finally, to some extent, it competes with other low-ticket entertainment
products such as baseball cards and video rentals. This problem can be
viewed in Table 2–2.

A similar approach can be used to define competitors for Federal
Express in the overnight package delivery market. Such a delineation
might be such as that shown in Table 2–3.

TABLE 2–2

Level of Competition	Definition	Competing Company	Need Satisfied
Product form	Diet colas	Coca-Cola	Low-calorie, nonalcoholic, cola-flavored carbonated beverage
Product category	Soft drinks	Hicks & Haas (who now own 7UP), Procter & Gamble	Nonalcoholic carbonated beverage
Generic	Food and beverages	Pillsbury (Burger King), Seagrams (wine), Perrier (bottled water)	Food and drink
Budget	Food and entertainment	3M (VHS tapes), Topps (baseball cards)	Enjoyment

TABLE 2–3

Level of Competition	Definition	Companies	Need Satisfied
Product form	Overnight air delivery	Emery, Purolator	Exact form transmission of material overnight picked up and delivered
Product category	Small package delivery	Eastern Airlines, UPS, U.S. Post Office	Rapid transmission of exact form
Generic	Transportation and transmission of information	AT&T, IBM/MCI, Telex, Southwest Airlines (People Movement)	Movement of parts and information
Budget	Provision of parts and information	Parts wholesalers and dealers, libraries	Provision of parts and information

It is also important to note that, as one moves from product form toward budget competition, the customer targets also begin to change. Product form competition suggests battling for exactly the same customers in terms of who they are and why they buy. (But not necessarily where or when they buy: one soft drink manufacturer may concentrate on fountain sales—Coke—and another on grocery store sales—Pepsi.) As you move toward budget competition, both who they are and why they buy begin to differ as the need satisfied becomes more general. Since the key to a business is customers, this suggests that the most crucial form of competition will *generally* be product form since they compete directly for *the same* customers. On the other hand, generic competition can destroy entire product categories when a major innovation occurs, and thus it, too, requires attention, especially for long-run planning.

It is important to note that those products which are thought of as substitutes, and therefore competitors, may also be viewed as complements, such as soda and hamburgers. When viewed this way, potential competitors can be turned into allies in various joint ventures (e.g., cooperative advertising). Thus, what this delineation of competitive levels does is define potential competitors and not necessarily mortal foes.

At this point it should also be clear that in the short run, product form and product category competition are generally most critical. Consequently, most annual plans focus on these almost exclusively. However, it seems foolish to not at least delineate more general forms of competition. To say differently, concentrating only on product form can allow a competitor to gain a massive share in a short period of time as a market shifts or a new technology appears (e.g., IBM's loss to Digital Equipment Company (DEC) in minicomputers and DEC's subsequent loss to Apple in microcomputers).

METHODS FOR DETERMINING COMPETITORS

The easiest way to define competition is to let someone else do it for you. Thus, the use of *existing categories* for frequently purchased goods or Standard Industrial Classification (SIC) codes for industrial products is popular and quite useful for uncovering exact form competition. However, since these methods are generally either product form or product category based, relying exclusively on these categories will overlook both generic and budget competitors.

Another way to define competitors is based on the *technical feasibil-*

ity of substitution. Here an engineering assessment suggests what other products could serve the same function as the one in question. However, this method does not explicitly take into account customer perceptions and consequently would overlook competition between, say, ice cream and soda.

There are basically two more alternative approaches to assessing the set of competitors facing a brand: managerial judgment and customer-based evaluation. We discuss them in some detail in the following text.

Managerial Judgment

Through experience, salesperson call reports, distributors, or other company sources, managers are often able to develop judgments about the sources of present and future competition.

One way of structuring the thought process is through the use of tabular material such as that shown in Table 2–4, which is a variant of Ansoff's (1965) well-known growth matrix. Box A represents product form competition; that is, those products or services that are basically the same and that are pursuing the same customers. Box C represents product form competitors who target other customers.

The most interesting cell of Table 2–4 is B. This cell represents potential future competitors who already have a franchise with our customers but do not offer the same product or service. In this case, the manager might try to forecast which firms falling into B are likely to become more direct competitors. Examples of this type of capitalization on prior customer familiarity with a company are numerous. If we consider telecommunications, IBM has a considerable franchise with large business customers through its mainframe computer business. IBM will

TABLE 2–4
Managerial Judgment of Competition

Markets	Product/Services	
	Same	*Different*
Same	A	B
Different	C	D

thus easily move to cell A through its purchases of MCI and Rolm. If we consider the orange juice market, Procter & Gamble has perhaps the best franchise of any consumer products manufacturer with both super-markets and consumers which it used to develop the Citrus Hill brand of orange juice. This type of movement is common in retail business where companies often try to use their "brand franchise" in one category to grab sales in others which serve the same customers (e.g., Nike's unsuc-cessful move into clothing). Through judgment, managers should assess the likelihood of such horizontal movements as well as their chances of success.

Cell D competitors are very difficult to predict as they currently sell different products to different markets. One example of the impact of such a competitor was Litton Industries' commercialization of microwave technology in the area of consumer durables which created a new com-petitor in the kitchen appliance market for General Electric.

Perhaps the least scientific but most useful way to see what a prod-uct or service might compete with is to imagine the item as a "prop" for a stand-up comedian. The comedian, unencumbered by convention (and sometimes good taste), can create many uses for a product, therefore suggesting different competitive products.

Customer-Based Measures

Two types of customer data are commonly used to assess competitive market structures: (1) actual purchase or usage data and (2) judgments (Day, Shocker, & Srivastava, 1979). While the former represent actual behavior, they are constrained by the fact that they indicate only what customers actually have done and not what they would have preferred to do in the past, or will do in the future. Thus, behavioral data are more useful for assessing current market structure than future.

Purchase-Based Measures

Several measures of competition based on past behavior have been pro-posed: (1) brand switching, (2) interpurchase times, and (3) cross-elastic-ity of demand. We will discuss these measures in detail.

Brand Switching
Probabilities of brand switching have been proposed as measures of customers' perceived similarities and, therefore, substitutability among

brands (Kalwani & Morrison, 1977; Lehmann, 1972). High brand switching probabilities thus imply a high degree of competition. A major drawback to brand switching measures is that the brands under consideration must be specified a priori which constrains the breadth of the competitive set of products. It is usually applied best in the determination of segment competitors for frequently purchased goods or services.

Another problem is that, as McAlister and Lattin (1983) argue, brand switches occur across complements as well as substitutes. Complements might be sought when consumers seek variety. For example, a consumer may become bored with Coke and switch to 7UP. A researcher would only observe a brand switch from Coke to 7UP for that consumer. Regardless of whether one attributed the switch to substitution or variety seeking, the revealed competitive structure would look quite similar.

Another problem with using purchase data is that most sources of it, such as panel data, are at the household level. Thus, switching between Diet Pepsi and Heineken might indicate whether the 13-year-old daughter or the older father made the purchase and not that soda and beer compete. Therefore, using actual brand switching data to define competition is useful but far from infallible.

Interpurchase Times

Using an interpurchase time criterion (Fraser & Bradford, 1983), two items are said to be perfect substitutes and, therefore, competitors if

$$E(X_{ii}) = E(X_{ij})$$

where $E(X_{ii})$ is the expected interpurchase interval for a repeat purchase of brand i, and $E(X_{ij})$ is the time interval between switching from i to j. Shocker, Zahorik, and Stewart (1984) evaluate this approach, which is only useful for frequently purchased items and is not widely used.

Cross-Elasticity of Demand

An estimate of the cross-elasticity of demand is the percentage change in one brand's sales with respect to a percentage change in another brand's price (or other marketing variable). If a cross-elasticity with respect to price is positive (i.e., a brand's sales decline when another brand's price drops), the two brands or products in question are considered to be competitive.

Several authors have used cross-elasticities to define markets (see Cooper, 1986). The major problem with this approach is the estimation of the cross-elasticities as it must be assumed that (1) there is no competitive reaction to the price cut, and (2) the market is static with respect to new entrants, product design, and so forth. As with brand switching measures, it is usually the case that the set of brands or products must be defined a priori.

In summary, the behavioral measures are useful in that they represent what customers actually do; they are not mere speculation. For the most part, however, they are only applicable to frequently purchased, nondurable goods. In addition, they tend to be most appropriate where a product class is defined a priori and what is being sought is a set of market definitions based on product form or category competition.

Customer Judgment-Based Measures

Four judgmental measures have been proposed (Shocker, 1986): (1) overall similarity, (2) similarity of consideration sets, (3) product deletion, and (4) substitution in use. Although not based on actual customer behavior, they have the advantages of providing insight into potential future market structures, producing broader definitions of current structures, and being applicable to all types of products and services including industrial products and consumer durables.

Overall Similarity

Judged similarity measures between products or brands can be used to create geometric representations in multidimensional spaces called *perceptual maps*. The brands or products are represented by points in the space, while the dimensions represent the attributes utilized by the customers in making the similarity judgments. Brands located close to each other are judged to be similar on the attributes and thus form a defined market.

For example, Figure 2-2 presents a perceptual map from the generic category of desserts. Although the analysis does (and must) begin with a prespecified set of alternatives, the set can be developed through focus group research emphasizing products satisfying a given need. The points not attached to the vectors represent the various products stated as filling the need for dessert. Information about the competitive sets is obtained by examining the clusters of points. The upper-right quadrant would be very useful to, say, the General Foods's brand manager for Jell-O. From the map, it is clear that Jell-O is perceived to be quite similar to custard, pudding, tapioca, Lo-Cal, and Dzerta. The vectors help to determine the

FIGURE 2–2
Defining Competition with Perceptual Mapping

Source: *Marketing News,* May 14, 1982, p. 3.

attributes defining the space but are not relevant to the market structure issue.

Similarity of Consideration Sets

An approach developed by Bourgeois, Haines, and Sommers (1979) asks customers to take a large set of products and divide them into piles representing those which are thought to be substitutable, that is, which would be considered together on a purchase occasion. The customers are then asked to judge the similarity of the products within each pile. By accumulating similarity judgments across the customers, a perceptual map can be developed. Thus, this approach is somewhat similar to the preceding one but collects the similarity judgments after the formation of consideration sets. Other variants of this approach use verbal protocol data (customers thinking aloud as they consider a decision).

Product Deletion

Urban, Johnson, and Hauser (1984) developed a market definition based on customer reaction to product unavailability. A set of products or brands are presumed to be substitutes and consequently form a market if, when one of them is deleted from the choice set, customers are more likely to buy from the remaining products than from a set of products outside the original set.

For example, suppose that a choice set for stereos consists of Pioneer, Sansui, and Technics. If, when Pioneer is eliminated from the set, customers are more likely to choose Sansui or Technics than McIntosh or any other brand, then the three brands are presumed to form a market.

Although described by authors as being primarily useful to partition product form markets into submarkets, there is no reason why the approach could not be used in a more general setting. For example, a choice set could consist of milk, orange juice, and soft drinks. If milk were unavailable and the orange juice and soft drinks were subsequently chosen more often than tea or coffee, then the milk, juice, and soft drinks apparently compete at the generic level.

Substitution in Use

Stefflre (1972) developed a procedure which is probably the most general in that it has the potential to uncover broad generic market definitions. Customers are first given the target product or brand and asked to develop a list of all its possible uses. Next, they are asked to list other products or brands that provide the same uses or benefits. Since, as might be expected, a large group of products results from these two steps, an independent sample of customers might be asked to rate the products on their appropriateness for the uses specified.

As an illustration, suppose the target product of interest is a checking account. A brief sketch of the analysis is provided below:

Target:	Checking account		
Uses:	Pay bills	Transactions	Security of money
Substitutes:	Pay by phone	Credit cards	Traveler's checks
Competitors:	AT&T	VISA	American Express

Thus, substitution in use can produce a set of fairly diverse competitors.

Summary

The methods for determining competition are summarized in Table 2-5 along two dimensions: (1) the usefulness of each method for determining competition at a certain level, and (2) the kind of research data typically used to implement the method. With respect to the latter, information is divided into primary sources (i.e., data collected specifically to determine competitors), and secondary sources (i.e., data collected for some general purpose other than to determine the structure of the market).

As can be seen from Table 2-5, all the methods are useful for determining product form competition. Managerial judgment and behavior-based customer data are mainly useful for developing product form and product category markets. Customer information that is judgment based, however, can be used to assess generic competition as well. Since cross-elasticities, similarity measures, product deletion, and substitution in use either start with an a priori market definition (although possibly very broad) or are usage based, they cannot really be used to define budget competition, that is, those products fighting for the same customer dollar. Since the consideration-set approach has no such restrictions, it can be used to assess budget competition.

With respect to data requirements, the judgment-based customer evaluations require primary data, while behavior-based methods can use secondary data. In particular, the latter methods often make use of consumer panel data which are records of household purchasing from a variety of product categories. Consumer judgments might supplement purchase data with primary data, such as interviews focusing on motivations for brand switching. Managerial judgment can (and at least implicitly does) utilize both primary (e.g., interviews with distributors) and secondary (e.g., salesperson call reports) data.

COMPETITOR SELECTION

While examining competition at four levels makes sense intuitively, the practical implications for the market manager are substantial. As mentioned earlier, one implication is that marketing strategy must be developed with an eye toward four different problems: (1) convincing customers in your segment that your brand is best (product form competition); (2) convincing buyers that your product form is best (product

TABLE 2–5
Methods versus Competition Levels and Information Required*

Approach	Level of Competition				Typical Data Sources	
	Product Form	Product Category	Generic	Budget	Primary	Secondary
Managerial judgment	X	X			X	X
Customer behavior based:						
Brand switching	X	X				X
Interpurchase times	X	X				X
Cross-elasticities	X	X	X			X
Customer evaluation based:						
Overall similarity	X	X	X		X	
Similarity of consideration sets	X	X	X	X	X	
Product deletion	X	X	X		X	
Substitution in use	X	X	X		X	

*An X indicates that either the method is useful for determining competition at that level or it employs data of a certain type.

category competition); (3) convincing buyers that your product category is best (generic competition); and (4) convincing buyers in your segment that the basic need your product fulfills is an important one. A manager must decide what percentage of higher budget to expend on handling each problem.

A second implication of the four levels of competition is that a selective competitor focus must be chosen. A manager cannot focus either analysis or actual strategy on each competitor in the market, however it is defined, due to limited available resources. For example, the problem of the Pioneer marketing manager described earlier is the selection of which other low-priced stereos, other stereos, or other entertainment forms (and, therefore, specifically against which manufacturers or service supplier) against which she or he should compete.

Deciding which competitors to focus on can be facilitated through the examination of three factors: (1) the time horizon of marketing plan being developed (short versus long run), (2) the stage of the product life cycle relevant for the product, and (3) the rate of change in the technology.

With respect to the time horizon of the plan, if it is a one-year operating marketing plan, competition should be defined on both product form and product-form category bases as they reflect the short-term competitive outlook. For example, in the short run, Sanka's major competitors are primarily other decaffeinated instant coffees and, secondarily, other instant or regular coffees. On the other hand, for longer-term plans, all four levels of competition are relevant with special emphasis placed on the generic level to identify important competitive threats.

The stage in the product life cycle may be relevant to defining competition because the breadth of view of the industry varies over time. At the early growth stages of a product, particularly a new technology, competition should be broadly defined (generically) since a large part of the marketing task is convincing customers to substitute a new product for an existing one that was satisfying the consumers' needs. On the other hand, in mature markets, the focus should generally be on product form and category competitors in order to best assess whether or not to stay in a market.

Finally, if the rate of technological change is rapid, competition should be conceived as broadly as possible. This is characteristic of the communications field as such diverse products as word processors, home computers, cable TV, and satellites compete for certain services. Alternatively, narrow definitions (i.e., product form) are sufficient where new technical advances occur less frequently, as with food products.

Given that the appropriate levels of competition have been selected (i.e., the market has been defined), attention shifts to choosing the relevant competitors on which to focus. This assessment requires an initial pass at competitor analysis. The factors determining which competitors are relevant are related to the forecasts of the brands' likely strategies which are the major outputs of competitor analyses. However, what are also critical are the resources the competitors can bring to bear in the market. This focus on resources highlights a final perspective on competition called *enterprise competition,* which must be addressed.

ENTERPRISE COMPETITION

Ultimately, brands do not compete against each other in a vacuum; the resources of a company are a key determinant of its vulnerability to a marketing strategy. Thus, while we have been examining competition in this chapter from the perspective of a brand or product, it is important to note that firm versus firm or enterprise competition involves selection of the competitors against which strategies are mounted.

As an illustration, consider the personal computer market. On a product form basis, Apple's MacIntosh competes against the IBM personal computer and personal computer AT™, Commodore's Amiga™, and Compaq's Deskpro™, among others. However, it is clear that not all competitors are created equal. When Apple tries to go head to head with IBM in the business market, it competes in terms of product features against IBM's personal computer and personal computer AT but also against the IBM Corporation's resources in terms of dollars, sales force, image, and willingness to support their products.

It is often difficult to understand brand level competition without understanding the broader context in which it occurs. For example, it is hard to understand the BIC versus Cricket lighter battle without recognizing the general competition between BIC and Gillette which includes razors and pens as well as lighters.

Enterprise competition is often characterized by asymmetries in competitive perspectives. For example, American Motors Corporation (AMC) undoubtedly views General Motors as a competitor, but the reverse is probably not true. This does not mean that the two corporations' product lines do not overlap, but that from the enterprise perspective, GM views Ford, Chrysler, and Toyota as more potent adversaries and thus stronger threats to its competitive position.

SUMMARY

In this chapter, we have argued that the set of competitors which pose a threat to a brand can be highly varied and come from a variety of industries. Therefore, a "market" is often dynamic and difficult to define. We have presented a framework to conceptualize competition and methods to help form ideas about the competitive set. Finally, we have discussed approaches to selecting competitors in terms of choosing the relevant levels and specific brands.

Essentially, we suggest that the competitors are those companies whose products or services compete for the same customer either directly through offering similar products or services (product form or category competition), indirectly through satisfying similar basic needs (generic competition), or in terms of budget. Clearly, one can develop an essentially infinite list of competitors. In general, for a short-run plan (e.g., one year) most of the effort should be directed toward exact-form and similar-form competitors with relatively little attention to products that will only gradually affect your sales (e.g., bottled water if you sell wine). The longer the range of the plan, the more attention should turn to less similar competitors, especially those who are strong and have or are developing technologies that could threaten your business (e.g., computers if you sell typewriters).

REFERENCES

Abell, Derek F. *Defining the Business.* Englewood Cliffs, N.J.: Prentice-Hall, 1980.

Ansoff, H. Igor. *Corporate Strategy.* New York: McGraw-Hill, 1965.

Bourgeois, Jacques D.; George H. Haines; and Montrose S. Sommers. "Defining an Industry." Presented at the ORSA/TIMS Conference on Market Measurement, Stanford, Calif., 1979.

Cooper, Lee G. "Competitive Maps: The Structure Underlying Asymmetric Cross Elasticities." Los Angeles: Graduate School of Management, UCLA, 1986.

Day, George S.; Alan D. Shocker; and Rajendra K. Srivastava. "Customer-Oriented Approaches to Identifying Product Markets." *Journal of Marketing* vol. 43 (Fall 1979), pp. 8–19.

Fraser, Cynthia, and John W. Bradford. "Competitive Market Structure Analysis: Principal Partitioning of Revealed Substitutabilities." *Journal of Consumer Research* 10 (June 1983), pp. 15–30.

Kalwani, Manohar U., and Donald G. Morrison. "A Parsimonious Description of the Hendry System." *Management Science* 23 (January 1977), pp. 467–77.

Kotler, Philip. *Marketing Management.* 5th ed. Englewood Cliffs, N.J.: Prentice-Hall, 1984.

Lehmann, Donald R. "Judged Similarity and Brand-Switching Data as Similarity Measures." *Journal of Marketing Research* 9 (August 1972), pp. 331–34.

Levitt, Theodore. "Marketing Myopia." *Harvard Business Review,* July–August 1960, pp. 45–56.

McAlister, Leigh, and James M. Lattin. "Identifying Substitute and Complementary Relationships Revealed by Consumer Variety Seeking Behavior." Working Paper no. 1487–83, Sloan School of Management, MIT, 1983.

Shocker, Allan D. "A Bibliography of Recent Work in Market Definition and Structure." Working Paper, Owen Graduate School of Management, Vanderbilt University, 1986.

Shocker, Allan D.; Anthony J. Zahorik: and David W. Stewart. "Competitive Market Structure Analysis: A Comment on Problems." *Journal of Consumer Research* 11 (December 1984), pp. 836–41.

Stefflre, Volney. "Some Applications of Multidimensional Scaling to Social Science Problems." In *Multidimensional Scaling: Theory and Applications in the Behavioral Sciences,* ed. A. K. Romney, R. N. Shepard, and S. B. Nerlove. Vol. III. New York: Seminar Press, 1972.

Urban, Glen L.; Philip L. Johnson; and John R. Hauser. "Testing Competitive Market Structures." *Marketing Science* 3 (Spring 1984), pp. 83–113.

The Wall Street Journal. "Fast-Food Slump Hits Industry Giants as More Competition Bites into Profit." April 22, 1986.

CHAPTER 3

INDUSTRY ATTRACTIVENESS
ANALYSIS

OVERVIEW

Whether approaching from a new or existing product perspective, an initial question asked before the planning process can even begin is whether the industry of interest is sufficiently attractive to warrant investment in it, either by your company, current competitors, or potential new constraints. This idea of industry or market attractiveness is so important that almost all strategic planning models utilize it at least partially. For example, the product portfolio of the Boston Consulting Group uses the market growth rate as a proxy for attractiveness. Other models (Abell & Hammond, 1979, chap. 5) utilize a two-dimensional strategic grid consisting of market attractiveness and business position.

What is needed is an assessment of the fundamentals of the industry being considered. Given that the industry has been defined (see Chapter 2), an essential component of the marketing planning process is an analysis of the potential for a firm to achieve a desired level of return on its investment.

Rarely will all the characteristics of an industry point in the same direction. As a result, markets that some firms find attractive will be of little interest to others. For example, most observers consider the market for standard memory computer chips to be a disaster due to declining sales, high cyclicity, overcapacity, and many other factors. However, France's Thomson SA recently purchased Mostek at a price far below book value because of the technological strength of the company. The fast-food industry is considered to be mature, but new concepts are continually being introduced (e.g., D'Lites) perhaps because of the vastness of the market.

This chapter examines those factors (summarized in Table 3–1) con-

TABLE 3–1
Industry Attractiveness Summary

Aggregate market factors:
   Market size.
   Market growth.
   Stage in product life cycle.
   Sales cyclicity.
   Seasonality.
   Profits.
Industry factors:
   Threat of new entrants.
   Bargaining power of buyers.
   Bargaining power of suppliers.
   Current industry rivalry.
   Pressures from substitutes.
   Industry capacity.
Environmental factors:
   Technological.
   Political.
   Economic.
   Regulatory.
   Social.

sidered important in assessing the underlying attractiveness of a market. There are three main areas of inquiry: basic aggregate market factors, industry factors relating to the major participants, and environmental factors. We will also discuss sources of information for the attractiveness analysis components and provide an illustration of such analyses.

AGGREGATE MARKET FACTORS

Market Size

Market size (measured in both units and dollars) is clearly an important criterion as it relates to the likelihood of a product obtaining revenues to support a given investment. Large markets also offer more opportunities for segmentation than small ones (see Chapter 5). Therefore, both large firms and entrepreneurial organizations might find large markets attractive. Large markets, however, tend to draw competitors with considerable resources, thus often making them unattractive for small firms. Witness the soft drink industry, for example. Thus, absolute size is not, by itself, sufficient to warrant new or continuing investment.

Market Growth

As mentioned previously, this is the key market factor advocated by the Boston Consulting Group. Not only is current growth important, but, because of the product life cycle, growth projections over the horizon of the plan are also critical. Fast-growing markets are almost universally desired due to their abilities to support high margins and sustain profits into future years. However, they also attract competitors. For example, while Sony developed the U.S. market for videocassettes, the projected high market-growth rate supported the entry of other firms marketing systems with a competing recording format (VHS) which now dominates Sony's Beta format.

Product Life Cycle

These two factors, market size and growth, are often portrayed simultaneously in the form of the product life cycle. Usually presumed to be S-shaped, this curve breaks down the sales of a product into four segments: introduction, growth, maturity, and decline. The introduction and growth phases are the early phases of the life cycle while sales are still growing, maturity represents a leveling-off in sales, while the decline phase represents the end of the life cycle.

The attractiveness of products in each of the phases of the life cycle is not always clear. Products in the growth phase, such as personal computers, are generally thought to be attractive. However, as Osborne, Commodore, and others have found out, high rates of market growth do not ensure success. Although mature markets are often disdained, clever marketers often find new ways to segment them which produce opportunities. Witness the successes of Miller's Lite beer and Minnetonka, Inc's Check•Up® antiplaque toothpaste. Finally, brands in declining product categories are also in an unfavorable position within the corporation. Harrigan (1980) gives several examples of strategies to turn the business around.

Sales Cyclicity

Since many firms attempt to develop products and acquire entire companies to eliminate interyear sales cyclicity, this is clearly not an attractive characteristic of an industry (unless, of course, it balances out cycles in other components of a firm's business). Highly capital-intensive business, such as automobiles, steel, and chemicals, are often tied to general business conditions and therefore suffer through peaks and valleys of sales as gross national product (GNP) and/or interest rates vary.

Seasonality

As is the case with sales cyclicity, seasonality, or intra-year cycles in sales are generally not viewed positively. For example, the toy industry has just lately reduced its reliance on the Christmas period to generate most of its sales. Such seasonal business tends to generate price wars since there may be little other chance to obtain sales revenues. However, on detailed scrutiny, most industries are seasonal to some extent (e.g., ice cream, beer, travel services, heating oil).

Profits

While there is certainly variability across products in an industry, there are also interindustry differences in profits. For example, the profit margins for the soft drink, drug, machine tool, and tire industries in 1985 were 15.1 percent, 22.7 percent, 6.6 percent, and 7.6 percent, respectively (Standard & Poors *Analyst Handbook,* 1986).

These differences in profitability across industries actually account for a variety of underlying factors. Differences can be due to factors of production (labor versus capital intensity, raw materials), manufacturing technology, and competitive rivalry, to name a few. Suffice it to say the industries that are chronically low in profitability are less attractive than those which offer higher returns.

A second aspect of profitability beyond the absolute level is their variability over time. Variance in profitability is often used as a measure of industry risk. Semiconductors offer abnormally high return when demand is good but concomitant poor returns when demand slumps. Food-related businesses, on the other hand, are known to produce steady if unspectacular profits. As is usually the case, there is a risk-return trade-off that must be made where the expected returns are evaluated against the variability in those returns.

We can summarize these variables as stated in Table 3–2.

INDUSTRY FACTORS

While the market factors just described are important indicators of the attractiveness of an industry, they do not provide any information about

TABLE 3–2

Variable		Attractiveness
Market size	High	+
	Low	−
Market growth	High	+
	Low	−
Sales cyclicity	High	−
	Low	+
Sales seasonality	High	−
	Low	+
Profit level	High	+
	Low	−
Profit variability	High	−
	Low	+

the industry's structure. Porter (1980) considers five factors in assessing the structure of industries:

1. Threat of new entrants.
2. Bargaining power of buyers.
3. Bargaining power of suppliers.
4. Current industry rivalry.
5. Pressures from substitutes.

A sixth factor, industry capacity, can also be considered in assessing industry structure.

Threat of New Entrants

If the threat of new entrants is high, the attractiveness of the industry is diminished. Except for the early stages of market development when new entrants can help a market to expand, new entrants bring additional capacity and resources which usually heighten the competitiveness of a market and diminish margins. Even at early stages of market growth, the enthusiasm with which new entrants are greeted is tempered by who the competitor is. For example, while Apple computers publicly welcomed IBM's entry into the personal computer market, it is unlikely that there was considerable private elation in Cupertino, California.

Key to the likelihood of new competitors entering a market are the barriers to entry which have been erected by the competition. We will now discuss some of the many potential barriers.

Economies of Scale.   An important barrier to entry into the automobile industry is the large plant size needed to operate efficiently, obtain quantity discounts on raw materials, and so on. Small manufacturers (e.g., Ferrari) must be content with serving the high-priced market segment. Economies of scale are obtainable in areas other than manufacturing. For example, hospital supply margins are better if many products are distributed since order-taking costs are largely fixed.

Product Differentiation.   Well-established brand names and/or company reputations can make it difficult for new competitors to enter. In the ready-to-eat breakfast cereal industry, the big four—Kellogg Co., General Foods, General Mills, and Quaker Oats—have such long-established reputations that a new competitor would find it difficult to establish a brand franchise.

Capital Requirements.   These requirements could be related to both manufacturing facilities and marketing. For example, a major use of capital in the fast-food industry is for advertising and sales promotion. Most of the high capital expenditures required to enter the farm equipment industry is for manufacturing facilities.

Switching Costs.   These are costs to buyers of switching from one supplier to another. If switching costs are high, such as they are in the mainframe computer business, it is difficult to convert a competitor's existing customers to you. In 1974, American Hospital Supply (AHS) installed order-taking terminals in the stockrooms of large hospitals. This created a barrier to potential new entrants as hospitals routinely ordered AHS supplies through its proprietary system.

Distribution.   Shelf space can be difficult for new products to obtain. The recent bifurcation of Coke into Classic and New Coke has raised this barrier to entry into the soft drink industry even higher as the two brands occupy more space than either one would alone. Similarly, some have argued that United's and American's airline reservation services provide an unfair advantage to those airlines.

What can also act as a barrier is the industry's willingness to vigorously retaliate against newcomers. When small Minnetonka Inc. innovated with a pump for hand soap, both Colgate and Procter & Gamble immediately copied the package and outspent Minnetonka in promotion. That story has been replayed in toothpaste.

It is also important to note that barriers can change over time. When Xerox's patent on its basic copying process expired, the number of competitors in the copier market dramatically expanded.

Bargaining Power of Buyers

The following diagram acts as a reference point for the purposes of discussing the power of both buyers and suppliers:

$$\text{Buyers} \longleftarrow \begin{array}{c} \text{Industry} \\ \text{of} \\ \text{concern} \end{array} \longleftarrow \text{Suppliers}$$

Thus, buyers are any people or institutions who receive finished goods or a service from the industry being analyzed. These could be distributors, OEMs, or end customers. Suppliers are any institutions that supply the industry of concern with factors of production, such as labor, capital, and machinery.

High buyer bargaining power is negatively related to industry attractiveness. In such circumstances, buyers can force down prices and play competitors off against each other for other benefits, such as service. Some conditions when buyer bargaining power is high are:

1. When the product bought is a large percentage of the buyer's costs: Historically the automobile industry has not had larger buyer power over the steel industry, at least partially, because steel is so important to car manufacturing. This power, however, is increasing as steel is replaced by plastics.

2. When the product bought is undifferentiated: If the industry of concern views what it sells as a commodity, buyers will have a great deal of power. A good example of this is the leverage held by customers of commodity chemicals.

3. When the buyers are earning low profits: Ailing industries such as farm equipment can extract better terms from supplier industries than can healthy industries such as food processing.

4. When there is a threat by the buyer to backward integrate:

Among other pressures felt by semiconductor manufacturers is the constant threat by computer manufacturers to make their own chips. IBM's purchase of Intel is such an example. Consumers also "backward integrate" as the growth of do-it-yourself hardware stores indicates.

5. When the buyer has full information: Consumers can exert more power in retail stores if they are fully aware of competitive offerings. For example, car dealers may be more willing to negotiate on price if the buyer signals that he or she is knowledgeable (Feldman & Winer, 1986).

In general, consumers are limited to their buyer power on an individual basis. (Notable exceptions exist, of course, such as the U.S. government as a purchaser of military equipment.) However, if consumers can be motivated as a group, they become a more important customer and thus exert more power than would otherwise be the case. For example, the highly desired dual-income couples in their 30s are considered to have large power since they are consumption oriented and may thus constitute a large portion of a seller's sales. Similarly, buying cooperatives have increased power.

Bargaining Power of Suppliers

This is really just the mirror image of the buyer power assessment. High supplier power is clearly not an attractive situation as it allows supplies to dictate price and other terms such as delivery dates to the buying industry. Some conditions when supplier bargaining power will be high are:

1. When suppliers are highly concentrated, that is, they are dominated by a few firms. Industries in need of supercomputers face strong suppliers since there are very few in the world.
2. When there is no substitute for the product supplied. The supercomputer falls into this category as well. By contrast, the power of OPEC has recently diminished as many industries converted plants to be able to use both oil and coal.
3. When the supplier has differentiated its product and/or built-in switching costs. Armco Inc. has increased its power with the automobile industry by offering General Motors a delayed payment plan for its steel, a guarantee of no work stoppages, a demonstration of how cheaper steel could be substituted in certain areas, and extra service by supplying steel already prepared with adhesives for certain applications.

Current Industry Rivalry

Industries that are characterized by intensive combat between the major participants may not be as attractive as those where the rivalry is on more sedate terms. Often, a high degree of rivalry results in escalated marketing expenditures, price wars, employee raids, and other related activities. Such actions can go beyond what is considered to be "normal" market competition and can result in decreased welfare for both consumers and competitors.

The recent "Battle of the Burgers" provides an illustration of this type of rivalry. Both McDonald's and Burger King, the major participants, drastically increased advertising budgets but did not deliver any increased value to customers. Now that equilibrium has been achieved, neither firm is better off in terms of profits, and Burger King is still looking for an ad campaign and position in the marketplace that will result in a permanent shift in its share.

Some of the major characteristics of industries exhibiting intensive rivalry are summarized below.

1. *Many or balanced competitors.* The fast-food, automobile, and soft drink industries would be characterized by each having several large, well-endowed competitors. The personal computer market, on the other hand, is dominated by IBM as most of the other competitors are either much smaller in size (Tandy, Apple, Commodore) or weaker in marketing (AT&T, ITT).

2. *Slow growth.* Again, fast food, autos, and soft drinks qualify. The relevant issue here is, of course, that in mature markets, growth can only come from another competitor.

3. *High fixed costs.* In such industries there is extreme pressure to keep operations running at full capacity in order to keep average unit costs down. For this reason, capital-intensive industries such as paper and chemicals are highly competitive.

4. *Lack of product differentiation.* Not only do basic commodities, such as aluminum, cattle, and chemicals, suffer from this problem, so do consumer products such as air travel. In fact, any industry where the basic competitive weapon is price probably suffers from a lack of differentiation and its concomitant extensive rivalry.

Pressures from Substitutes

Industries making products or delivering services for which there are a large number of substitutes are less attractive than those which are delivering a relatively proprietary service. Since almost all industries suffer from the availability of substitutes, this may not be a determinant characteristic of an unattractive industry. However, some of the highest rates of return are earned by industries in which the range of substitutes is low. For example, as mentioned earlier, the drug industry, in which few legal substitutes are available, earns a profit margin of 22.7 percent.

Determining the degree to which substitutes exist would be related to how the industry is defined. If it is defined generically (see Chapter 2), then all substitutes already define the industry. If it is defined on a product-form or category basis, then the number of substitutes could be determined using a method described in Chapter 2.

Industry Capacity

A final characteristic to observe is the historical supply and demand situation in the industry. Chronic overcapacity is not a positive sign for long-term profitability. When an industry is operating at capacity, its costs stay low and its bargaining power with buyers is normally high. Thus, often a key indicator about the health of an industry is whether there is a consistent tendency toward operating at or under capacity.

TABLE 3–3

Industry Factor		Attractiveness
Threat of new entrants	High	−
	Low	+
Power of buyers	High	−
	Low	+
Power of suppliers	High	−
	Low	+
Rivalry	High	−
	Low	+
Pressure from substitutes	High	−
	Low	+
Unused capacity situation	High	−
	Low	+

Summary

The industry analysis can be summarized as shown in Table 3–3.

ENVIRONMENTAL FACTORS

Consider the following diagram of the relationship of a firm to its environment. A definition of environment might include those factors outside the control of both the firm and its industry. The susceptibility of an industry to changes in the environment is an unattractive characteristic. As mentioned earlier in this chapter, if an industry's sales are tied to the domestic economic situation, cyclicity can result. On the other hand, industries that are well positioned to take advantage of environmental changes may prosper.

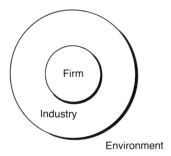

Environmental factors to be examined can be put into five groups: technological, political, economic, regulatory, and social. These factors should be examined not only to assess industry attractiveness but also to determine if any forecasted changes in these areas dictate changes of strategy.

Technological Factors

Figure 3–1 displays a model of the technological environment which is useful for conceptualizing sources of technological change in an industry (Thomas, 1974). The "technology" and "impetus" dimensions are self-explanatory. The "process" dimension draws distinctions between the development of new products (invention), the introduction of that product (innovation), and the spread of the product through the population (diffusion).

FIGURE 3–1
Typology of Technical Developments

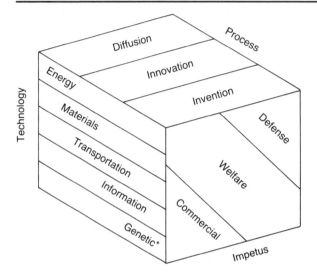

*Includes agronomic and biomedical developments.
Source: Philip S. Thomas, "Environmental Analysis for Corporate
Planning," *Business Horizons* 17 (October 1974), p. 27.

Two key dimensions that should be used to assess an industry's attractiveness are technology and process. With respect to the former, major changes are occurring in the energy, materials, transportation, information, and genetic (bioengineering) areas. With respect to information, for example, the scanning systems installed at the cash registers in supermarkets enable the retailers to closely monitor sales of different items for both inventory and shelf-space allocation decisions. Bioengineering research is being used to both improve crop yields and find cures for various diseases, including cancer.

Industries that are not strong on the technology dimension are particularly vulnerable to competition both from new industries and from foreign competitors that have made the necessary investment. Most major steel firms use the blast furnace technology developed in the 1800s. Foreign steel firms and those domestic companies who invested in modern manufacturing technology have been highly successful in the past decade.

There is, however, a point beyond which technology can create a backlash, particularly among consumers. Naisbitt (1984) refers to this as "high-tech versus high touch." For example, the move by banks to install automatic teller machines has depersonalized banking to the point where some consumers yearn for the human contact afforded by tellers. Several years ago, Citibank in New York proposed to allow only its wealthiest customers to have personal contact for most transactions while others were forced to use machines. Consumers protested so vehemently that Citibank scrapped the idea.

Attractive industries are also strong in either the invention, innovation, or diffusion of new products or services. Most consumer products companies must continually innovate since the life cycles for many frequently purchased consumer goods are short. By contrast, the cigarette industry has had difficulty, in general, both launching and developing new products, although this is interrelated with regulatory problems.

Political Factors

A second environmental factor relates to the industry's sensitivity to political factors. These are particularly relevant for products that have substantial foreign markets. Table 3–4 conceptualizes the sources of political risk, the groups through which political risk can be generated, and the political problems on the operation of the business.

For example, one of IBM's major markets is South Africa. Following Table 3–4, the sources of political risk are both social unrest and disorder and internal struggles for power. The groups responsible for the risk are largely nonorganized common interest groups. One effect on IBM's business would be possible damage to property and personnel from riots. However, another impact (not listed in Table 3–4) is the potential loss of goodwill in other countries who resent IBM's doing business in South Africa.

While such an analysis does not imply assessing a whole business such as personal computers as being unattractive, it aids in the evaluation of geographically defined market segments. In addition, if a sufficient percentage of a business's sales came from risky foreign markets, such a business could, in fact, look unattractive relative to others.

Domestic U.S. political risk is generally not as great, but still important. It is usually related to which political party is in power. Republicans tend to favor free market economies. Therefore, industries hardpressed by foreign competition (e.g., shoes, textiles) would probably not receive any relief through quotas or tariffs. Democrats, tending to favor some market intervention, might favor not only some of the above programs

TABLE 3–4
Conceptualizing Political Risks

Sources of Political Risk	Groups through Which Political Risk Can Be Generated	Effects on International Business Operations
Competing political philosophies (nationalism, socialism, communism) Social unrest and disorder Vested interests of local business groups Recent and impending political independence Armed conflicts and internal rebellions for political power New international alliances	Government in power and its operating agencies Parliamentary opposition groups Nonparliamentary opposition groups (Algerian "FLN," guerilla movements working within or outside country) Nonorganized common interest groups: students, workers, peasants, minorities, and so on Foreign governments or intergovernmental agencies such as the EEC Foreign governments willing to enter into armed conflict or to support internal rebellion	Confiscation: loss of assets without compensation Expropriation with compensation: loss of freedom to operate Operational restrictions: market shares, product characteristics, employment policies, locally shared ownership, and so on Loss of transfer freedom: financial (dividends, interest payments, goods, personnel, or ownership rights, for example) Breaches or unilateral revisions in contracts and agreements Discrimination such as taxes or compulsory subcontracting Damage to property or personnel from riots, insurrections, revolutions, and wars

Source: Stefan H. Robock, "Political Risk: Identification and Assessment," *Columbia Journal of World Business,* July–August 1971, p. 7.

but also an industrial policy that would benefit the industries selected to be a part of it. Defense spending and, hence, the fortunes of defense-related industries also have this type of political risk.

Economic Factors

A wide variety of factors fall into this category. Of particular interest is the sensitivity of the industry of concern to these economic factors.

1. *Interest rates.* Almost all capital goods industries (machine tools, computers) are sensitive to interest rate fluctuations since their high costs to buyers are often financed at short-term rates. Consumer durables such as homes, cars, and stereos, are also sensitive to interest rates, although consumer credit rates do not react as much to changes in the prime lending rate as do commercial rates.
2. *Exchange rates.* Again, the impact of having foreign markets or producing in other countries can vary widely over time depending on currency exchange rates.
3. *Unemployment rates.* Since service businesses often hire relatively unskilled labor at low wage rates, they are highly dependent on employment conditions. When employment rates are high, for example, fast-food employees are hard to find as higher-paying jobs are available. The conditions of demand and supply of labor for each industry must be considered as well. The supply of engineers is cyclical. When supply is down, many firms in technically related businesses suffer from a shortage of skilled labor.
4. *GNP.* Industries that have broad customer bases (machine tools, copiers) are often sensitive to fluctuations in GNP growth. When the country is in a recession, so are these industries. This cyclicity mentioned earlier in this chapter is not an attractive feature of an industry.
5. *Inflation rates.* These are, of course, tied in with interest rate fluctuations and, as a result, have a similar impact.

Regulatory Factors

Government and other agencies have an impact on industry attractiveness through regulations. Some industries have become less attractive over time because of laws passed which restrict their abilities to market or raise the overall cost of doing business. The cigarette industry, for example, has had restrictions placed on media which can be used for advertising. The mining, steel, and auto industries have all been affected by environmental laws.

It is not possible to generalize about the sources of regulatory impact as each industry is affected by different regulatory bodies. As a result, this part of the analysis must be highly industry specific.

Social Factors

Trends in demographics, lifestyles, attitudes, and personal values among the general population are of particular concern for consumer products manufacturers for several reasons. First, new products have been developed to fit into today's lifestyles. Frozen entrées, for example, were developed to suit dual-career households with a need for convenience and easy preparation at dinnertime. Second, new features have been added to existing products. More upper-income households have ice cream makers in refrigerators, fancy stereos in cars, and telephones with built-in calculators and a memory for holding frequently called numbers. Finally, promotion has changed as well. How often do we see the "Yuppie" on television ads?

What is not generally recognized is the importance of understanding trends in lifestyles for industrial product industries. Since the demand for industrial products is often derived demand (i.e., generated ultimately by consumers), changes in the source of that demand can clearly affect demand for the end product. For example, when car demand slumps, so does the demand for steel, plastic, aluminum, and other industries heavily dependent on the auto industry.

For consumer businesses, the key question to ask is whether the industry under consideration is well positioned to take advantage of current trends. Some product areas that are "hot" because they appeal to the fast-growing "baby boomer" group are furniture and electronic appliances, upscale fast-food chains, clothing, financial and travel services, and upscale baby accessories. Industries having trouble are colleges, coffee, cigarettes, and brown alcohol because they are being buffeted by either demographic or taste trends.

For industrial companies, the key question to ask is whether *the customers* of the industry being considered are in the "right" industries. Clearly, firms supplying the "hot" industries above will do well, while those which are heavily tied to declining consumer products will not. The industrial problem, then, is customer selection.

Summary

In this section, we have attempted to identify the major factors in the environment related to industry attractiveness. While each major factor is too complex to conveniently summarize, it is clear that important information concerning the long-term prospects for an industry lie outside its control.

It should also be stressed that the environmental analysis should also be used to help develop strategy for a product. While we have emphasized using environmental data to assess an industry's future health, it can and should be used to plan new products and product improvements and for market segment selection.

DATA COLLECTION

The analysis of industry attractiveness is summarized in Table 3-1 in the first section of this chapter. Here we will recap the main points as previously discussed. The aggregate market factors are pieces of information all firms should have regarding its businesses. The industry factors are more qualitative, except for the capacity data. Most of these can be obtained through observation of the relevant markets or speaking with industry participants. For example, the extent of industry rivalry is easily observable from the actions of the firms. Therefore, both the market and industry factors are easily obtainable from standard industry sources.

The environmental data present a different case. Many trends in the environment are not readily available from industry sources since trend-spotting involves both data collection and analysis.

One approach is to hire a professional trendspotter. Several firms specialize in collecting and analyzing environmental data for client firms. These include the Naisbitt Group (Washington, D.C.), Inferential Focus (New York), Perception International (Connecticut), and Weiner Edrich Brown (New York). For fees ranging from $10,000 to $30,000 per year, these firms provide reports and personal consultations.

The alternative to hiring a consultant is to design an environmental scanning function within the company. A committee can be set up and composed of managers representing different functional areas of the firm. The duties of the committee would be to essentially replicate the activities of the consulting firms. The consultants generally are voracious consumers of printed media. Popular scanning resources are national and regional newspapers, journals reporting new scientific developments

(*Psychology Today, Scientific American*), "fringe" literature (*Mother Earth News, Heavy Metal*), and trend-tracking publications (*the Futurist, World Future Society Bulletin*). The committee would be charged with clipping and abstracting relevant items, summarizing the data into a small number of key issues, and finally recommending strategies to deal with the issues. Environmental analysis is basically an information collection process where the sources of information are as disparate as possible.

Example

As an example of the preceding discussion, Table 3–5 has been developed from information obtained about the instant camera market. The example was developed about 1984, prior to Kodak's forced exit from the market. As can be seen, the market was basically a duopoly with only Kodak and Polaroid, largely the latter, competing for a total market of 6.7 million units (now, of course, Kodak has been legally forced out of the instant camera market). The information presented in Table 3–5 is meant to be illustrative of what could be done in assessing the attractiveness of an industry and is not necessarily complete.

In terms of the aggregate market factors, the market is mixed. It exhibits good growth but not high profitability. In addition, the heavy seasonality implies a complication from a manufacturing standpoint.

From an industry analysis perspective, some of the factors are positive. The threat of new entrants is low, and the bargaining power of both buyers and suppliers is not high. However, the rivalry between Kodak and Polaroid is intense, and, perhaps more importantly, there are many substitutes both in existence and being developed.

Finally, except for the foreign exchange risk, the environmental factors appear to be positive, particularly the social/demographic factors.

To be able to shift the analysis from qualitative to quantitative, a firm employing this scheme would have to develop both importance weights for the factors and an evaluation scale for the information derived for each factor. For example, constraining the importance weights to sum to 1 within a major grouping, threat of entry, and bargaining power of buyers and suppliers might receive .15 each while threat of substitutes .30 and rivalry .25. If a 5-point scale was employed on the information where the numbers are increasing with respect to the attractiveness of the information, then the threat of entry and bargaining power of buyers might both get 5; power of suppliers 3; and substitutes

TABLE 3–5
Industry Attractiveness Summary: Instant Camera Market (1984)

Major market participants: Kodak (25 percent), Polaroid (75 percent)

Aggregate market factors:
1. Market size: 6.7 million units.
2. Market growth: 15 percent average (1982–84).
3. Product life cycle: declining.
4. Sales cyclicity: negligible.
5. Profits: moderate; about 9 percent margins.
6. Seasonality: substantial.

Industry factors:
1. Threat of new entrants: low.
2. Barriers:
    a. Distribution
    b. R&D expenditures.
    c. Backward integration.
    d. Patents.
    e. Other capital.
    f. Economies of scale.
3. Bargaining power of buyers: low:
    a. Few manufacturers.
    b. Traffic builders to retailers.
4. Bargaining power of suppliers: medium:
    Firms are backward integrated but key is silver for film which fluctuates in supply.
5. Current industry rivalry: high:
    Polaroid is particularly committed to the market.
6. Pressure from substitutes: high:
    a. 35 mm cameras.
    b. "One-hour" photo developing labs.
    c. Video cameras.
7. Industry capacity: unknown.

Environmental factors:
1. Technological:
    a. Many in photography market creating new substitutes.
    b. Changes in industry relate to speed of film developing, quality of pictures.
2. Political:
    Important foreign exchange risks (Polaroid established Monetary Control Center in 1983 to try to control exposure).
3. Economic:
    Currently in a growth period for disposable income, inflation easing.
4. Regulatory:
    Decision in 1985 forcing Kodak to abandon the business, patent infringements suits.
5. Social:
    a. More first births → need for pictures.
    b. Increased leisure time.

and rivalry 1. The score for the instant camera market in terms of the industry analysis would then be .15 × 5 + .15 × 5 + .15 × 3 + .30 × 1 + .25 × 1 = 2.5. Scores would also be computed for the aggregate market and environmental factors, added together, and compared to other markets or norms developed over time. Abell and Hammond (1979, chap. 5) present a similar weighting scheme.

The weights or perspective in general used in evaluating the factors would be highly dependent on whether the firm is already competing in the industry or is contemplating entering it. For example, the profitability of an industry would be more important to a firm which has not committed to enter than to an existing competitor which faces exit barriers.

SUMMARY

This chapter has presented a framework for analyzing industry attractiveness. The three major sets of factors to consider are aggregate market factors such as market size and growth, industry factors such as power of buyers and suppliers, and environmental factors such as demographic and regulatory trends.

REFERENCES

Abell, Derek F., and John S. Hammond. *Strategic Market Planning.* Englewood Cliffs, N.J.: Prentice-Hall, 1979.

Feldman, David, and Russell S. Winer. "Price-Setting under Asymmetric Information and Random Signaling Cost." Working Paper no. 38/85–86, Graduate School of Management, Carnegie-Mellon University, 1986.

Harrigan, Kathryn Rudie. *Strategies for Declining Businesses.* Lexington, Mass.: Lexington Books, 1980.

Naisbitt, John. *Megatrends: Ten New Directions for Transforming Our Lives.* New York: Warner Books, 1984.

Porter, Michael E. *Competitive Strategy.* New York: Free Press, 1980.

Robock, Stefan H. "Political Risk: Identification and Assessment." *Columbia Journal of World Business,* July–August 1971, p. 7.

Standard & Poor's. *Analyst Handbook.* New York: Standard & Poor's Corporation, 1986.

Thomas, Philip S. "Environmental Analysis for Corporate Planning." *Business Horizons* 17 (October 1974), p. 27.

CHAPTER 4

COMPETITOR ANALYSIS

OVERVIEW

In Chapter 2, we discussed the determination and selection of competitors against which the marketing plan will be focused. Assuming this process has been completed, the next step is to analyze the competitors in order to better formulate a marketing strategy which acknowledges the competitors' likely actions. As Porter (1979) has said, "The essence of strategy formulation is coping with competition."

Competitor analysis has received more attention in the last few years for several reasons. First, many product categories can be characterized as being mature businesses in that growth rates are declining. In such markets, competitive pressures are intense as gains in unit sales volume are derived from the other firms; that is, the market can be described as a zero-sum game. As a result, firms which understand their competitors' possible future strategies have an advantage over those which tend to be inward oriented.

A second impetus to competitor analysis has come from the fact that product life cycles are shortening (Booz Allen & Hamilton Inc., 1982). Accordingly, there is more pressure on product managers to recoup investments made in a shorter period of time which makes errors of judgment about competition difficult to overcome.

Finally, the last decade has been perhaps the most turbulent period ever faced by marketing managers because of increased foreign competition, dramatic changes in technology and rates of innovation, large shifts in interest rates and inflation, and changing customer tastes. When the environment contains so much uncertainty, it is important to keep abreast of changes in all factors exogenous to the firm, including competition.

Some companies, of course, have discovered the importance of competitor analysis. Some examples are:

IBM has a commercial analysis department with thousands of branch office representatives responsible for reporting information about the competition.

Texas Instruments has employees analyze government contracts won by competitors to discern their technological strengths.

Citicorp has an executive with the title "manager of competitive intelligence."

McDonald's distributes Burger King and Wendy's Competitive Action Packages to its store managers.

Wang has analysts whose jobs are to track competitor software development.

Why don't all firms have a formal reporting system designed to collect and analyze information about competitors? First, overconfidence about a product's continued success can reduce the willingness to collect competitor information. However, an impressive list (General Motors, Coca-Cola, McDonald's) of such manufacturers who were somewhat overconfident at one time can be produced along with the competitors who were ignored until they made significant inroads into the markets (Toyota, Pepsi, Burger King). A second reason given for being insensitive to competition is uncertainty about where to collect the necessary information and how to analyze it. This excuse is becoming weaker all the time as consultants specializing in competitive intelligence-gathering articles containing tips on where to collect information, and computerized databases containing articles about companies become more widespread.

A final reason for not collecting competitive intelligence is an ethical consideration—the fear that either illegal methods or otherwise "dirty" tricks have to be used to obtain such information. Many examples of such behavior exist. "Reverse" engineering (copying) is a popular method in technology industries for shortening lead times in introducing "me-too" products. Running phony help wanted ads in order to lure and hopefully question competitors' employees is another frequently used ploy. However, it is almost always the case that information obtained in such a manner can be ethically obtained.

What is necessary to analyze competitors is a commitment to developing competitive strategy which includes a willingness to expend resources collecting such data. However, the data itself are usually not the major problem facing marketing planners. As stated earlier, there are many sources of competitor intelligence. What is often lacking is a structure to guide the collection and analysis of the data, a clear idea of what questions the data should address.

In this chapter, a structure is proposed for collecting, organizing, and analyzing competitor information. There are four areas of interest as stated here.

1. What are the competitors' major objectives?
2. What is the current strategy being employed to achieve the objectives?
3. What are the capabilities of the competitors to implement their strategies?
4. What are their likely future strategies?

The last aspect of competitor analysis could be called the bottom line. The purpose of examining the competitors is to be able to forecast what they are likely to do over the next planning cycle. As mentioned previously, a marketing strategy for a product must account for these likely future strategies. The first three parts of the analysis are the background data needed to predict the future strategies. Together, these four areas of information collection and analysis compose a fairly complete picture of the competitors' activities.

ASSESSING THE COMPETITORS' CURRENT OBJECTIVES

The first step in competitor analysis is to attempt to assess what the current objectives are for the major competitor brands. An assessment of current objectives provides valuable information concerning the intended aggressiveness of the competitors in the market in the future. It also provides a context within which the capabilities of the competitors can be assessed; that is, does the firm marketing Brand A have the resources to successfully pursue such an objective?

When discussing the idea of objectives, it is important to define precisely what is meant by the term since there are many different types of objectives. In the context of marketing planning, three basic brand objectives can be identified.

1. *Growth Objective.* This usually implies growing the brand in terms of either units or market share with profit conditions being secondary.

    2. *Hold Objective.*   This could also be termed a consolidation ob-
jective. A hold scenario might be logical for a brand which is
losing market share, in that a reasonable first step in reversing its
fortunes is to put a brake on the slide.

    3. *Harvest Scenario.*   This could also be termed a *milking* objec-
tive. Here, profit is of paramount importance.

In other words, at the brand level, objectives are typically stated in
terms of either market share or profits. At the corporate level, return on
investment or other more aggregate statistics become more relevant.

Determination of Competitor Objectives

While a brand's objective determines to a great extent what strategies will
be pursued and, hence, what actions will be taken in the marketplace,
usually it does not take a substantial amount of research to uncover it.
What is required is sensitivity to competitors' actions through observation, salesperson call reports, and so on.

    Let us consider the two major options outlined above—the growth
versus harvest choice. If a competitor's brand is being pushed to improve
its market position at the expense of short-term profits, then some of the
following are likely to occur.

    1. A cut in price.
    2. Increased advertising expenditures.
    3. Increased promotional activity both to consumer and trade.
    4. Increased distribution expenses.

In other words, a firm that is trying to expand a brand's market share will
be actively spending money on market-related activities and/or reducing
price. Such actions can be easily monitored by the brand managers,
advertising account representatives, and other parties with access to information about the rival brand's actions.

    Brands being harvested would be marketed in the opposite way. An
increase in a competitor's price, decreases in marketing budgets, and so
on, can be interpreted as a retreat (perhaps only temporary) from active
competition in the market. While exact estimates of the size of the share
loss expected cannot be obtained, it is not difficult to establish the
direction of the objective which is the important competitive information.

    Two other factors are relevant to the assessment of competitors' objectives. First, the objectives of a foreign brand or a product marketed by a firm with a foreign parent are often affected by the country of origin. In many cases, such firms have financial backing from a government or major banks and are not as concerned with short-term losses as they are with establishing a viable market position or obtaining foreign currency. Thus, depending on the competitor, cues concerning the competitor brand's objectives can be obtained from the geographical home of the parent firm.

A second relevant factor is whether the ownership of the competitor firm is private or public. Since the former do not have to account to stockbrokers, long-term profits may be more important than showing positive quarterly returns. On the other hand, if a family depends on the firm for current income, profits may be more important than market share. In these cases, knowledge of the ownership situation provides vital cues concerning the objectives that are likely to be pursued.

A less apparent level of objectives can be deduced from a firm's operating philosophy and procedures. For example, a firm that seeks to minimize capital investment will be slow to respond to a competitor that makes a heavy capital outlay (e.g., as Emery Air Freight was when Federal Express bought their own planes in the mid-1970s). Similarly, firms that compensate their sales staff based on a percent of sales commission indicate that volume (rather than profitability) is a key objective. In fact, the key performance measure (e.g., return on fixed assets) often has a distinct influence on a firm's behavior.

In sum, estimates of the objectives pursued by competitors provide important information for the development of strategy. Certainly, a brand that is being aggressive in its pursuit of market share must be viewed as a different type of competitor than one that is primarily attempting to maximize profits. The latter brand would clearly be vulnerable to an attack against its customers, while a confrontation with the former brand might be avoided. In other words, a study of the brands' objectives provides a first-level analysis of how to evaluate the competitor brands.

This type of analysis has been profitably applied. During the late 1970s, Coca-Cola was primarily concerned with holding market share and improving profits. Pepsi, on the other hand, viewed Coke's drowsiness as an opportunity and became more aggressive, gaining share points and improving its position versus Coke, which it still maintains. Miller's successful attack on Budweiser during the 1970s was prompted by a similar observation.

ASSESSING THE COMPETITORS' CURRENT STRATEGIES

The second stage in competitor analysis is to determine how the competitors are attempting to achieve their objectives. This question is addressed through an examination of their past and current strategies.

Marketing Strategy

Many authors have attempted to define the concept of strategy. At the brand level, a marketing strategy can be thought of in terms of three major components:

1. Target market selection.
2. Core strategy (i.e., differential advantage).
3. Implementation (i.e., supporting marketing mix).

The first major component is the description of the market segment(s) to which the competing brands are being marketed. Market segments can be described in various ways, as shown in Table 4–1. (See also Chapter 5.) Since few brands are mass marketed (i.e., marketed to all potential customers), the key point here is to determine which group(s) each brand has targeted. This is important from the perspectives of (1) avoiding segments where there may be intense competition, and (2) determining undertargeted segments which may represent opportunities.

The second strategy component is what is called the core strategy (Luck & Prell, 1968). This is the basis on which the rival is competing,

TABLE 4–1

Variables	Typical Breakdowns
Geographic:	
Region	Pacific; Mountain; West North Central; West South Central; East North Central; East South Central; South Atlantic; Middle Atlantic; New England.
County size	A; B; C; D.
City or SMSA size	Under 5,000; 5,000–19,999; 20,000–49,999; 50,000–99,999; 100,000–249,999; 250,000–499,999; 500,000–999,999; 1,000,000–3,999,999; 4,000,000 or over.
Density	Urban; surburban; rural.
Climate	Northern; southern.

TABLE 4–1 *(concluded)*

Variables	Typical Breakdowns
Demographic:	
Age	Under 6; 6–11; 12–17; 18–34; 35–49; 50–64; 65 +.
Sex	Male; female.
Family size	1–2; 3–4; 5 +.
Family life cycle	Young, single; young, married, no children; young, married, youngest child under 6; young, married, youngest child 6 or over; older, married, with children; older, married, no children under 18; older, single; other.
Income	Under $5,000; $5,000–$7,999; $8,000–$9,999; over $10,000.
Occupation	Professional and technical; managers, officials and proprietors; clerical, sales; craftspeople, supervisors; operatives; farmers; retired; students; housewives; unemployed.
Education	Grade school or less; some high school; graduated high school; some college; graduated college.
Religion	Catholic; Protestant; Jewish; other.
Race	White; black; Asian.
Nationality	American; British; French; German; Eastern European; Scandinavian; Italian; Spanish; Latin American; Middle Eastern; Japanese; and so on.
Social class	Lower-lower; upper-lower; lower-middle; middle-middle; upper-middle; lower-upper; upper-upper.
Personality:	
Compulsiveness	Compulsive; noncompulsive.
Gregariousness	Extrovert; introvert.
Autonomy	Dependent; independent.
Conservatism	Conservative; liberal; radical.
Authoritarianism	Authoritarian; democratic.
Leadership	Leader; follower.
Ambitiousness	High achiever; low achiever.
Values	SRI VALS Typology (Mitchell, 1983), Rokeach's 18 terminal and instrumental values (1973); List of Values (Kahle, 1986).
Buyer behavior:	
Usage rate	Nonuser; light user; medium user; heavy user.
Readiness stage	Unaware; aware; interested; intending to try; trier; regular buyer.
Benefits sought	Economy; status; dependability.
End use	Varies with the product.
Brand loyalty	None; light; strong.
Marketing-factor sensitivity	Quality; price; service; advertising; sales promotion.

that is, its key claimed differential advantage(s). This is a critical component of strategy as it usually forms the basic selling proposition around which the brand's promotion is formed. It could also be called the brand's *positioning.*

Brand managers essentially have a choice between two types of differential advantages: price/cost based and product-feature based. In other words, brands are usually positioned on price or quality dimensions. Concentration on price follows the classic approach developed by the Boston Consulting Group (Henderson, 1980) which advocates taking advantage of the experience curve which drives down unit costs and provides the ability to cut prices and maintain margins over time. While cost cutting does not necessarily imply declining prices, the brand wishing to claim a differential advantage based on price must be in a competitively superior position in terms of unit costs. The quality differential advantage, heavily advocated by Peters and Austin (1984), is a claim to be superior on some other product dimension, such as service, packaging, and terms of delivery. Necessary conditions for such a core strategy to be successful are that customers value the characteristics claimed as advantages and that the differential can be maintained for a significant period of time without being copied.

An important characteristic of quality differential advantages is that they can often be perceived rather than actual differences. For example, IBM's core strategy since its inception has been service based. This is an actual differential advantage because it can be supported by hard data (e.g., number of field service representatives, mean response time, and so on). On the other hand, Pepsi's claimed differential over Coke relates to its "younger generation" appeal; that is, drink Pepsi if you want to drink what younger people drink. Such positioning is clearly outside the domain of physical product differences but is nonetheless effective in differentiating Pepsi from Coke. Physical product differences are often stressed in industrial, durable, or new frequently purchased product strategies. Mature, frequently purchased products that are physically similar or "commodities" often emphasize perceptual differences.

The final strategy component of competitors which must be assessed is the supporting marketing mix. The mix provides insight into the basic strategy of the competitor as well as information-relevant specific tactical decisions. The areas to consider and some questions to consider follow.

Pricing

Pricing is a highly visible element of a competitor's marketing mix; therefore several questions can be addressed. For example, if a brand's differential advantage is price based, is the list price uniform in all markets? If the strategy is quality based, what is the price differential claimed? Are discounts being offered? In general, any price-related information pertaining to the implementation of the aforementioned strategy is relevant.

Promotion
With respect to sales management, what kinds of selling approaches are being employed? Are the salespeople being aggressive with respect to obtaining new accounts? In terms of advertising, what media are being used? What creative strategies? What timing pattern? Sales promotion questions are also important, for example, which types and how often?

Distribution
Have the channels of distribution shifted? Is the brand being emphasized in certain channels? Is the manufacturer of the competing brand changing the entire system; for example, by opening its own retail outlets?

Product
Have any product features been changed? Have any improvements been made in packaging?

How to Assess Competitors' Strategies

It should be emphasized at this point that detailed information about competitors is not yet necessary. Up to this stage in the competitor analysis process, all that is required are qualitative assessments of objectives and strategies. As a result, in attempting to ascertain competitors' current strategies, it is unnecessary to develop detailed information.

Recall that the two key elements of a strategy are the segments appealed to and the core strategy. For industrial products, both can be easily determined by an examination of three sources of information: company sales literature, your own sales force, and trade advertising. The former provides information about the core strategy as brochures usually go into detail concerning points of difference to be emphasized regarding the firm's product versus those of competitors. Even if a specific table is not provided comparing the product in question to competitors' products on several dimensions, the sales literature should indicate the brand's major strengths. A firm's own sales force can provide some data concerning companies or industries being targeted. Much of this is of an informal nature resulting from contacts, trade show discussions, and the like. Finally, trade advertising is useful for both the segments being targeted and the differential advantage touted. The latter can be determined directly from the copy while the former can be at least partially determined by the publication in which the ad appears.

For consumer goods, simply tracking competitors' ads provides most of the information necessary. Television ads can be examined in terms of message (differential advantage) and program (target segment[s]). TV advertising is quite useful for the determination of the core strategy since the nature of the medium prohibits the communication of all but the most important messages. Similarly, print advertising can provide equivalent information but with more elaboration concerning the core strategy.

For example, consider the copy for a print ad for 1-2-3® from Lotus® shown in Figure 4–1 obtained from *Fortune* magazine. At least part of Lotus's strategy can be determined by utilizing both the fact that the ad appeared in *Fortune* and the copy itself. The target market for this ad can be determined from (1) demographics of *Fortune's* readership, and (2) the copy, which illustrates a business application of the software. The claimed differential advantage is the additional productivity obtainable by using Lotus. This is only part of the overall strategy for the product since other ads could be oriented toward different segments with possibly different claimed advantages.

Information concerning the implementation of the current strategies is also easily found. Pricing-related information can be obtained from basic market observation; that is, distributors, salespeople, customers, advertising agencies, or even a firm's own employees acting as consumers on their own behalf, can be the sources of pricing data. Promotion, distribution, and product-related facts can be obtained from similar sources. In other words, as in the case of objective determination, it takes only market sensitivity to assess much of the competitive activity occurring rather than sophisticated management information systems.

One very apparent but often overlooked source of information is being a customer and/or stockholder of the competitors. Both customers and stockholders get special mailings and information which makes strategy assessment easier. Furthermore, personal use of competitors' products often gives one a feeling for them which does not come through even the best prepared research. Thus policies that forbid the use of competition products are usually foolish.

FIGURE 4–1
Determining Strategy from Print Ads

"Before 1-2-3 we used to guess."

A major California vineyard could never quite match the demand for their wines to their annual crop yield.

Two years ago they began using 1-2-3® to more accurately predict vineyard harvests by grape variety. Now they have the right grapes to produce more of their best-selling wines.

A real estate developer who used to guess at how a change in the amortization schedule, interest rates or the tax code would affect cash flow on her properties, now uses 1-2-3.

Now she knows for certain.

A large mail-order house specializing in outdoor clothing and equipment once relied on instinct to develop new products for their customers.

Now they rely on 1-2-3. Last year, they generated a 30% increase in sales.

A major cranberry cooperative has a better handle on crop yields, inventory and fruit harvests since using 1-2-3.

A leading insurance company has tighter control over relocation expenses for transferred executives using 1-2-3.

There's a surgeon in Boston who has developed a better way to monitor his patients' vital signs using 1-2-3.

A large southern utility has better control over the distribution and pricing of its natural gas.

An airline now keeps better track of passenger miles thanks to 1-2-3.

How much good could 1-2-3 do for your business?

At this point, you can only guess.

"1-2-3. The ultimate business tool."

This year an estimated one million people will discover how much more productive they can be using the premier spreadsheet, graphics and database software: 1-2-3 from Lotus.®

1-2-3 from Lotus is the best tested, best supported, most proven personal computer business software in the world. And we've just made it even better with new 1-2-3.

Shouldn't you be using it?

© 1985, Lotus Development Corporation. 1-2-3 and Lotus are registered trademarks of Lotus Development Corporation.

Technological Strategy

An important task is to assess the technological strategies of the major competitors, that is, how they approach market conditions. This can be done using the framework of Maidique and Patch (1978) who suggest that six decisions need to be made.

1. Technology selection or specialization.
2. Level of competence.
3. Sources of capability: internal versus external.
4. R&D investment level.
5. Competitive timing: initiate versus respond.
6. R&D organization and policies.

These decisions generally lead to four basic strategies, each of which has different requirements for success (see Table 4–2).

At this point in the analysis it is often useful to summarize the products of the major competitors. Table 4–3 provides a general format which is useful both for summarizing the results and for communicating them. More will be said on assessing the market segmentation part of Table 4–3.

ASSESSING COMPETITORS' CAPABILITIES

It is assumed that evidence has been accumulated thus far concerning competitors' current objectives and strategies. Recall that the ultimate goal of this analysis is to predict the competitors' likely future strategies. Thus, the bridge between what they are doing now and what they are likely to do in the future is the current and likely future state of health of the competing brands and their manufacturers.

What to Collect

Several frameworks have been proposed to indicate which information to collect about competitors (Ansoff, 1979; Hussey, 1971). One that has been used extensively was developed by Rothschild (1979). He divides the necessary information into five mutually exclusive categories concerned with the competitors' "abilities." These categories are discussed below.

Ability to Conceive and Design
This category attempts to measure the quality of the firms' new-product development efforts. Clearly, a firm with a high ability to develop new products is a more serious long-term threat in a product category than a firm which has not been innovative.

Ability to Produce
In this category, we attempt to determine the production capabilities of the firms. For a service business, this category might be termed *ability to*

TABLE 4–2
Typical Functional Requirements of Alternative Technological Strategies

	R&D	Manufacturing	Marketing	Finance	Organization	Timing
First to market	Requires state-of-the-art R&D	Emphasis on pilot and medium-scale manufacturing	Emphasis on stimulating primary demand	Requires access to risk capital	Emphasis on flexibility over efficiency; encourage risk taking	Early-entry inaugurates the product life cycle
Second to market	Requires flexible, responsive, and advanced R&D capability	Requires agility in setting up manufacturing medium scale	Must differentiate the product; stimulate secondary demand	Requires rapid commitment of medium to large quantities of capital	Combine elements of flexibility and efficiency	Entry early in growth stage
Late to market or cost minimization	Requires skill in process development and cost effective product	Requires efficiency and automation for large-scale production	Must minimize selling and distribution costs	Requires access to capital in large amounts	Emphasis on efficiency and hierarchical control; procedures rigidly enforced	Entry during late growth or early maturity
Market segmentation	Requires ability in applications, custom engineering, and advanced product design	Requires flexibility on short to medium runs	Must identify and reach favorable segments	Requires access to capital in medium or large amounts	Flexibility and control required in serving different customers' requirements	Entry during growth stage

TABLE 4–3
Format for Competitive Product Analysis

	Competitor A Brand 1...K_A	Competitor B Brand 2...K_B
Product:		
Quality		
Features		
Target segment:		
Who		
Where		
When		
Why		
Place:		
Distribution method		
Distribution coverage		
Promotion:		
Total effort ($)		
Methods		
Advertising:		
Strategy/copy		
Media		
Timing		
Total effort (B)		
Price:		
Retail		
To trade		
Technological strategy		

deliver the service. For example, a firm that is operating at capacity for a product is not as much a threat to expand in the short run as is a firm that has slack capacity, assuming a substantial period of time is required to bring new capacity on-line.

Ability to Market
How aggressive, inventive, and so on are the firms in marketing their products? A competitor could have strong product development capabilities and slack capacity but be ineffective at marketing.

Ability to Finance
The availability of financial resources clearly acts as a constraint to being an effective competitor. While financial ratios are key pieces of informa-

tion, how the competitor firm shifts its resources between products is also critical.

Ability to Manage

Several years ago, Procter & Gamble replaced the manager of its U.S. coffee business with the coffee general manager from the United Kingdom. This new manager had a reputation for developing new products: in a 15-month period, for example, he oversaw the launch of four new brands, which was above average for the company. The message to competitors such as General Foods was clear. In general, the characteristics of key managers provide signals to competitors concerning strategies that are likely to emerge.

Examples of specific bits of information that should be collected are shown in Table 4–4. While the list is not exhaustive, it highlights the major areas that should be researched.

Where to Find the Information

The search for information necessary to cover the areas indicated in Table 4–4 is extensive. Typically, the search involves the collection of both primary (i.e., data not already collected by some other institution) and secondary data.

A good reference for secondary research sources including computer databases is a book by Stewart (1984). A brief listing of some of those sources is given in Table 4–5. The computer database information will be expanded upon in Chapter 7. In addition, recent books by Fuld (1985) and Sammon, Kurland, and Spitalnic (1984) discuss data collection specifically for competitor analysis in more detail.

An interesting dimension of the table is the breakdown of who does the "talking." Clearly, much of what can be determined about competitors' resources can be obtained from the firms themselves. For example, a firm will give away information about a future new plant location in a want ad seeking job applicants. A company that boasts about new products in an article in the business press gives rivals enough lead time to copy it. Plant tours are often good sources of information for competitors. Some companies, however (such as Kellogg), are eliminating such tours as defensive measures.

Why are competitors themselves often good sources of information? One explanation is that they do not take adequate defensive postures to prevent other competitors from obtaining sometimes critical information.

TABLE 4–4
Examples of Competitor Information to Be Collected

A. Ability to conceive and design:
   1. Technical resources:
      a. Concepts.
      b. Patents and copyrights.
      c. Technological sophistication.
      d. Technical integration.
   2. Human resources:
      a. Key people and skills.
      b. Use of external technical groups.
   3. Funding:
      a. Total.
      b. Percentage of sales.
      c. Consistency overtime.
      d. Internally generated.
      e. Government supplied.
B. Ability to produce:
   1. Physical resources:
      a. Capacity.
      b. Plant.
         (1) Size.
         (2) Location.
         (3) Age.
      c. Equipment.
         (1) Automation.
         (2) Maintenance.
         (3) Flexibility.
      d. Processes.
         (1) Uniqueness.
         (2) Flexibility.
      e. Degree of integration.
   2. Human resources:
      a. Key people and skills.
      b. Work force.
         (1) Skills mix.
         (2) Union.
C. Ability to market:
   1. Sales force:
      a. Skills.
      b. Size.
      c. Type.
      d. Location.
   2. Distribution network:
      a. Skills.
      b. Type.
   3. Service and sales policies.
   4. Advertising:
      a. Skills.
      b. Type.

TABLE 4–4 *(concluded)*

     5. Human resources:
       a. Key people and skills.
       b. Turnover.
     6. Funding:
       a. Total.
       b. Consistency overtime.
       c. Percentage of sales.
       d. Reward systems.
D. Ability to finance:
     1. Long term:
       a. Debt/equity ratio.
       b. Cost of debt.
     2. Short term:
       a. Line of credit.
       b. Type of debt.
       c. Cost of debt.
     3. Liquidity.
     4. Cash flow:
       a. Days of receivables.
       b. Inventory turnover.
       c. Accounting practices.
     5. Human resources:
       a. Key people and skills.
       b. Turnover.
     6. System:
       a. Budgeting.
       b. Forecasting.
       c. Controlling.
E. Ability to manage:
     1. Key people:
       a. Objectives and priorities.
       b. Values.
       c. Reward systems
     2. Decision making:
       a. Location.
       b. Type.
       c. Speed.
     3. Planning:
       a. Type.
       b. Emphasis.
       c. Time span.
     4. Staffing:
       a. Longevity and turnover.
       b. Experience.
       c. Replacement policies.
     5. Organization:
       a. Centralization.
       b. Functions.
       c. Use of staff.

TABLE 4–5
Representative Sources of Information about Competitors

	Public	Trade/Professionals	Government	Investors
What competitors say about themselves	Advertising Promotional materials Press releases Speeches Books Articles Personnel changes Want ads	Manuals Technical papers Licenses Patents Courses Seminars	Security and Exchange Commission reports FIC Testimony Lawsuits Antitrust	Annual meetings Annual reports Prospectuses Stock and bond issues
What others say about them	Books Articles Case studies Consultants Newspaper reporters Environmental groups Consumer groups Unions "Who's Who" Recruiting firms	Suppliers/vendors Trade press Industry study Customers Subcontractors	Lawsuits Antitrust State and federal agencies National plans Government programs	Security analyst reports Industry studies Credit reports

A firm that does not actively scan its competitors' activities may not be sensitized to defending itself. Alternatively, a firm taking active positions in terms of information dissemination about itself could be doing it consciously for several reasons. First, it could be trying to give signals to competitors both as a warning ("this is my turf") or to deceive. Second, the information is often "marketed" to security analysts and other elements of the financial community who either trade the company's stock, determine its creditworthiness, or provide capital. Finally, the information has value for the morale of employees who tend to prefer working for a firm that is visible and dynamic.

What to Do with the Information

This is the stage at which many competitor analysis efforts fall flat. What do we do with all the information that is collected? What is necessary is a useful format for synthesizing the large quantity of information at hand.

A first step toward making some sense out of all the data is to construct a table of the information patterned after that shown in Figure 4-2. This forces the manager to "boil" down the information to its essential parts and provides a quick summary of a large amount of data. Note that one column of the table is labeled "Yourself." This forces what is termed *an internal assessment* in that the firm performing the analysis ultimately must see how its resources compare with those if its competitors.

Figure 4-3 is presented as a matrix illustrating this data simplification. As can be seen, all the information previously prescribed cannot be gathered in a limited period of time. In addition, quite often qualitative assessments and estimates based on partial information must be made.

However, even the illustration in Figure 4-3 can be further simplified. This entails (1) determining key factors for success in the business in question, and (2) based on the data from Figure 4-2, rating the competitors along those key factors or dimensions.

As can be seen from Figure 4-4, while Xerox had some key strengths in the late 1970s, it was particularly vulnerable on price/cost and reliability dimensions. Thus, a two-step data reduction approach results in a clarified picture of the competitive situation and relatively clear directions for strategy development.

Assessing a Competitor's Will

Even the strongest competitor can be overcome if it is not committed to the market. Similarly, even a weak competitor can cause massive damage if it is fanatically committed.

FIGURE 4–2

	Firm				Yourself
	A	B	C	D	

Conceive and design:
- Technical resources.
- Human resources.
- Funding.
-
-
-
-

Produce:
- Physical resources.
- Human resources.
-
-
-
-

Finance:
- Debt.
- Liquidity.
- Cash flow.
- Budget system.
-
-
-

Market:
- Sales force.
- Distribution.
- Service and sales policies.
- Advertising.
- Human resources.
- Funding.
-

Manage:
- Key people.
- Decision process.
- Planning.
- Staffing.
- Organization structure.
-
-

FIGURE 4–3
U.S. Competitor Matrix for Copiers (c. 1979)

Competitors' Analysis	Xerox	Savin	Canon	Remaining Significant Japanese Competition
Ability to conceive and design new products:				
R&D budget	$376.3 MM	$4.597 MM	$33 MM	Unknown
Historical record	Poor	Very good	Excellent	Very good
Human resources	Improving	Good	Good	Good
Patent filings	Very good	Good	Excellent	Very good
Trademarks	Excellent	Good	Excellent	Very good
In-house development versus licensing	In-house	Contracted	In-house	In-house/license
Ability to manufacture or produce:				
Capacity	Improving	Nil	Excellent	Very good
Lead time	Improving	Long	Excellent	Very good
Control of resources	Very good	Nil	Very good	Very good
Labor problems	Under control	None	None	None
Age of plant and condition	Mixed	None	Modern	Modern
Location	Excellent	None	Japan	Mixed
Cost	Good	Very good	Excellent	Very good
		(Vulnerable to currency fluctuation)		
Location on experience curve	Excellent	None	Excellent	Very good/improving

FIGURE 4-3 (concluded)

Competitors' Analysis	Xerox	Savin	Canon	Remaining Significant Japanese Competition
Ability to market:				
Advertising budget	$5.6 MM	$3.4 MM	$.9 MM	$2.2 MM
No. of salesmen	Excellent	Good	Average	Good
Inventories	Medium	Small	Small	Variable
Philosophy	Improving	Excellent	Very good	Good
Dealer networks	Direct	Very good	Good	Good
Distribution points	Well located	Well located	Fair located	Good located
Ability to finance:				
Cash position	Excellent	Poor	Good	Mixed
Risk due to exchange fluctuation difficulties	Nil	Large	Large	Mixed
Long-term/short-term debt	0.54	1.4	0.26	Mixed
Moody's ratings	Aa	B	N.A.	Ba
Ability to manage:				
Historically	Poor but improving	Excellent	Excellent	Very good
Chief executive officer	Commitment	Entrepreneur	Old but consumer oriented	Mixed

FIGURE 4–4
Competitive Analysis Simplification: Copier Market

	Companies			
Criteria	Xerox	Savin	Canon	Remaining Japanese Competitors
Low price and operating costs	(3)	(4)	(2)	(1)
Reliability of equipment	(4)	(1)	(2)	(3)
Widespread effective distribution	(1)	(4)	(2)	(3)
Good R&D facilities	(1)	(4)	(2)	(3)
Financial strength	(1)	(4)	(2)	(3)
Reputation	(1)	(2)	(3)	(4)
Placement offerings	(1)	(2)	(4)	(3)

Note: (1) = Best.

At some point, it is crucial to assess the competitor's strength of will or commitment. This requires going beyond objectives (What do they want?) to assess the intensity with which they approach the task (How badly do they want it?). Most competitions involve several key times at which point each competitor has the choice of backing down or continuing the fight. In assessing the likelihood of a competitor continuing the fight (an act which sometimes is not "rational" in a profit sense), one should assess:

1. How crucial is this product to the firm? The more crucial in terms of sales and profits, number of employees, or strategic thrust, the more committed most companies will be to it. This helps explain why efforts to unseat a market leader by attacking the heart of their market provoke violent reactions ("If those _____ think they can take our market without a fight, . . .") whereas a strategy which nibbles away at secondary markets is more likely to go unmatched ("Well, it only represents 2 percent of our sales, so we shouldn't be too concerned about it").

2. How visible is the commitment that has been made to the market? It may be difficult to admit you are wrong. A good example

of this is Exxon's Office Systems Division which was clearly in trouble for a long time before it was sold in 1985.
3. How aggressive are the managers? Personality differences exist and some people are more combative than others. The most combative opponents react with a fervor which makes reaching a business detente almost impossible.

Only by knowing how badly a competitor "wants it" can we successfully approach the next task, predicting future strategies.

PREDICTING FUTURE STRATEGIES

The manager is now armed with three sets of information about his or her major competitors. First, we have assessed what their likely objectives are; that is, for what reward they are currently playing the game. Second, we have a view on their current strategy. Finally, we have some idea about their resources and abilities to compete. The final step is to put it all together and answer the question we started with: What are they likely to do in the future? In particular, we are interested in their likely strategies over the subsequent planning horizon, often a year.

One way to predict competitors' strategies does not employ the previously discussed information. Sometimes, the competitors will actually disclose their likely future strategies through sources previously listed in Table 4–4. For example, Warner-Lambert (*Advertising Age,* 1982) indicated that for its over-the-counter health care products, including Myadec vitamins and Benylin cough syrup, it was going to redirect promotion from health care professionals alone to include consumers as well. This indicated a clear shift in strategy—a change in market segments to which it was appealing.

Often, however, the competition does not come right out and indicate what strategies they will pursue. In that case, subjective estimates are based on the information previously collected and analyzed. One way to approach the problem is to emulate what forecasters do with historical data. With historical observations on both a dependent variable to predict (in our context, a competitor's strategy), and independent variables useful to predict the dependent variable (in our context, the resource variables), the forecaster might do one of two things. First, she or he might simply assume the trend will continue; that is, suppose that the only relevant information is the historical pattern of past strategies. For example, if a firm had a track record of selling brands with a premium image and high price, one could "extrapolate" into the future and assume this will continue. Similarly, if a brand has been appealing to increasingly mature consumers, a manager might presume that the trend will continue. This trend approach takes for granted that there is no information in the independent variables.

An alternative way for the forecaster to proceed is to try to establish a relationship of cause and effect between the resource variables and the strategy. In other words, an attempt could be made to link changes in resources or abilities to the strategies to be pursued.

Several examples will help clarify this approach. Several years ago, Merrill Lynch spent heavily to bring in managers with package goods experience to develop the markets for their financial services. Competitors (E. F. Hutton, Dean Witter) could forecast that this would result in an emphasis on market segmentation (pursuing high-potential customers) and increased spending on marketing-related activities such as advertising. Bethlehem Steel has invested billions of dollars in the last few years to upgrade its flat-rolled steel facilities. Competitors can forecast that this investment in highly efficient capacity will improve Bethlehem's ability to simultaneously cut price and protect margins. RCA tried for years to sell its Hertz subsidiary (it finally in the mid-1980s sold it to UAL, now Allegis Corporation). This resulted in RCA diverting marketing funds from Hertz to "fatten up" its bottom line and make it look more attractive to a potential buyer. Competitors of Hertz were, of course, delighted since it decreased Hertz's ability to market and therefore limited its strategic options. Finally, both Bell Labs and Du Pont have spent considerable resources training employees in the marketing concept suggesting a change in direction.

A third approach to strategy forecasting does not explicitly employ historical data but makes use of it in a different way. Corning Glass's highly profitable Corning Ware line was coming off patent. At the same time, it was well known that several companies (Libby-Owens-Ford, Anchor Hocking) were looking at that business. Corning was interested in how a competitor would enter in order to preempt the entry strategy. To forecast the probable entry strategy, it asked senior managers to role-play (i.e., simulate) a competitor and determine how, if they were managing the entry, they would attack Corning Ware. This exercise clearly provided useful defensive information to Corning.

Thus, a third approach to forecasting competitors' possible actions is to simulate them. One can take the existing data already collected, play

FIGURE 4–5
Game Theory Illustration

Payoff matrix

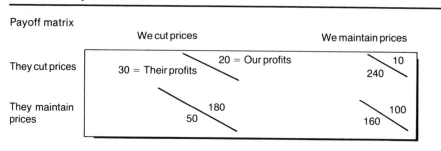

the role of the competitor, and develop competitor action scenarios. Smith Kline did exactly that when Tagamet, the largest-selling prescription drug in the world and the source of one third of Smith Kline's profits, was coming off patent. In this case, it knew who the competitor was going to be (Glaxo Holdings); Smith Kline prepared its salespeople concerning how they expected Glaxo to promote its drug, Zantac, in terms of differential advantage (fewer doses needed per day) and how to counteract arguments against Tagamet. This simulation approach has been highly effective in application.

When there are a small number of competitors, it is possible to use a combination of game theory and decision trees to predict competitive behavior. To use these we assume that the objective of both firms is known and the same, such as annual profits. Then for a particular decision, such as cut versus maintain current prices, we can calculate the profitability to both parties as shown in Figure 4–5, which represents a "game" between the two competitors. Here we see that total profits are maximized if both maintain prices. Notice, however, that both parties are better off cutting prices if their competitor maintains them. This makes the situation inherently unstable and also makes prediction of competitor strategy crucial to maximizing profits.

In response to this situation, it is apparently in the best interest of both parties to collude to maintain prices and, if they are sophisticated, to divide the extra profits they gain proportionally to their respective gains. Assuming such a cartel is illegal or unstable, the key to understanding behavior is often to assume that one competitor moves first and the other responds. For example, the decision tree in Figure 4–6 depicts the situation where we move first and the competitor responds. Given the estimated response probabilities (which should be based on the competitor analysis), we can compute the results of the two decisions:

FIGURE 4–6
Conditional Strategy Probabilities

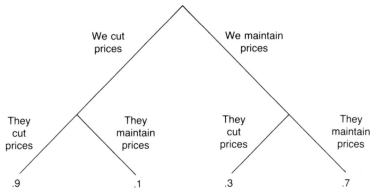

$$
\begin{aligned}
\text{We cut price} \quad &= \ .9 \ (20) \ + \ .1 \ (180) \ = \ 36 \\
\text{We maintain price} \quad &= \ .3 \ (10) \ + \ .7 \ (100) \ = \ 73
\end{aligned}
$$

Therefore, allowing competitive response leads to the conclusion that, on average, we would be better off maintaining price.

While building decision trees is clearly a correct way to proceed, it is quite unwieldy given multiple competitors and the many possible strategies that could be employed. Moreover, the probabilities needed are at best estimates. Consequently, as a first cut it is often useful to simply predict the basic strategy of competitors. This can be done as is suggested in Figure 4–7. Then, assuming we are contemplating an unexpected strategy, we can simply indicate the likely reactions of the competitors to various strategic alternatives as in Figure 4–8. While Figures 4–7 and 4–8 are much less elegant than either game theory or decision tree analysis, they are both easier to use and a more appropriate reflection of the typical level of information available for competitor analysis.

SUMMARY

The analysis of competitors is a crucial element in preparing a sensible marketing plan. Only by knowing what the competitors are likely to do can a firm hope to chose an optimal strategy. Essentially, competitor analysis involves: (1) assessing their objectives, (2) determining their cur-

FIGURE 4–7
Expected Competitor Behavior

	Product Form Competitors		Product Category Competitors	
	Diet Coke	"Price"—Diet Colas (Vintage, C&C, . . .)	Coke	7UP
Objective				
Strategy				
Mix elements:				
Product				
Price				
Advertising				
Promotion				
Distribution				

FIGURE 4–8
Expected Competitive Response

	Product Form Competitors		Product Category Competitors	
	Diet Coke	"Price"— Diet Colas	Coke	7UP
Environmental change:				
Overall demand				
Regulatory				
Competitive strategy change:				
1. (e.g., new product)				
2. (e.g., price cut)				

rent strategies, (3) evaluating their capabilities, and (4) forecasting their future strategies. This is the marketing equivalent of scouting, both in person and by studying the film, in sports. Given the effort put into scouting in such diverse sports as high school football and America's Cup racing, where the financial gain is limited, it seems only reasonable that a company dealing with a multimillion dollar product would want to be at least as well prepared.

REFERENCES

Ansoff, H. Igor. *Corporate Strategy.* Hammondsworth, Eng.: Penguin Books, 1979.

Booz Allen & Hamilton Inc. *New Products Management for the 1980s.* 1982.

Fuld, Leonard M. *Competitor Intelligence.* New York: John Wiley & Sons, 1985.

Giges, Nancy, and Gay Jervey. "W-L Plans Major Outlays," *Advertising Age,* May 3, 1982, p. 3.

Henderson, Bruce D. "The Experience Curve Revisited." *Perspectives,* no. 220. Boston: Boston Consulting Group, 1980.

Hussey, D. E. *Introducing Corporate Planning.* Oxford, Eng.: Pergamon Press, 1971.

Kahle, Lynn. "Alternative Measurement Approaches to Consumer Values: The List of Values (LOV) and Values and Life Styles (VALS)." *Journal of Consumer Research* 13 (December 1986), pp. 405-9.

Luck, David J., and Arthur E. Prell. *Market Strategy.* New York: Appleton-Century-Crofts, 1968.

Maidique, Modesto A., and Peter Patch. "Corporate Strategy and Technological Policy." Working Paper, Harvard Business School, 1978.

Mitchell, Arndt. *The Nine American Life Styles.* New York: Warner Books, 1983.

Peters, Thomas J., and Nancy Austin. *A Passion for Excellence: The Leadership Difference.* New York: Random House, 1985.

Porter, Michael E. "The Structure within Industries and Companies' Performance." *Review of Economics and Statistics* 61 (May 1979), pp. 214-27.

Rokeach, Milton. *The Nature of Human Value.* New York: Free Press, 1973.

Rothschild, William E. *Putting It All Together.* New York: AMACOM, 1979.

Sammon, William L.; Mark A. Kurland; and Robert Spitalnic. *Business Competitor Intelligence.* New York: John Wiley & Sons, 1984.

Stewart, David W. *Secondary Research.* Beverly Hills, Calif.: Sage Publications, 1984.

CHAPTER 5

CUSTOMER ANALYSIS

OVERVIEW

Customers are central to the practice of marketing since without customers, a business cannot survive. While this may appear to be clear, many marketing managers have regretted not obtaining sufficient information about their customers in order to develop products or strategies which are consonant with their needs.

A recent example is IBM's competitive battle with Digital Equipment Corporation (DEC). IBM has been struggling in the minicomputer market due to DEC's success with its VAX series, and from an unwillingness to allow its different-sized machines to communicate with each other. In the mid-1980s IBM had begun to listen to its customers by designing a machine, the 9370, which is superior to the VAX series in price and performance. IBM is also offering better warranties and more programming assistance, and is developing a standard architecture which will permit its machines to communicate with each other. In addition, IBM has (*Business Week,* March 30, 1987) agreed to keep large accounts informed about its product developments, something it had previously declined to do for proprietary reasons.

This chapter describes some ways to structure an analysis of customers. Before proceeding, it is important to note that in this chapter the term *customer* refers not just to current customers of a given firm but to both customers of competitors and current noncustomers of the product class. For useful planning to occur, it is important to consider the potential market for the product and not just its current market and customers.

It is also important to recognize that rarely will a single typical customer exist. Rather, it is likely that each customer is to some degree unique. Since it is usually both time-consuming and not profitable to develop a strategy for each customer, some grouping of customers into segments will be required. This segmentation is the compromise between treating each customer as unique and assuming all customers are equal. Its purpose is to both provide insights and make more efficient marketing programs.

This chapter proceeds by first discussing possible bases for describing customers. Next, a brief discussion of segment formation techniques is included. Then the concept of customer value, a key input into market potential estimation, and strategy determination, is discussed. Finally, a way to summarize the customer analysis is provided.

WHAT WE NEED TO KNOW ABOUT CUSTOMERS

The best basis for customer analysis is the one that leads to the best decisions and therefore greatest profit. Since this is a fairly vacuous tautology, a manager is faced with deciding on a basis he or she thinks will be useful. The following text is not necessarily an exciting but hopefully useful description of the most widely used bases (see Figure 5–1 for the overview).

Who Buys and Uses the Product

When a manager decides to analyze the customers in a market, the first question is, "Who are the customers?" For most industrial goods and many consumer goods, the "who" must be broken into (*a*) who buys it and (*b*) who uses it (the ultimate consumer), the identities of which may be widely different. One pertinent example is purchases made by a purchasing agent. Here the end user may be an engineer who is mainly concerned with cost and reliability of delivery. One reason for the success of Federal Express was their ability to bypass the shipping clerk in the decision on how to send overnight packages by making the user into the purchaser. Similarly, the purchase of cereal, toys, or fast-food meals is often made by an adult, whereas the user of the product is a child. McDonald's ads clearly recognize this and attempt to target both the teenage market (with money of their own) and the "family meal" break segment, where the child is likely to suggest going out to eat. This distinction also holds for goods sold for resale either directly or as a part of another product. In short, it is important to analyze both the immediate and ultimate customer.

FIGURE 5–1
What We Need to Know about Potential Customers

1. Who they are:
   a. Who is the purchaser?
   b. Who is the user?
2. What they do with it:
   a. What they buy?
   b. What they do with it?
3. Where they buy it:
   a. Information services/shopping location.
   b. Purchase location.
4. When they buy:
   a. Time of year.
   b. On versus off promotion.
5. Why they buy:
   a. Basic need.
   b. Specific attributes.
6. How they buy:
   a. Amount.
   b. Terms.
   c. Selection procedure.
7. Benefits:
   a. Currently obtained.
   b. Desired.

It is also important to identify all the parties to a decision, which can include both people and company policies. This means identifying the members of the buying center in industrial markets and members of the family in consumer purchase decisions who can impact the decision. Impact can take many forms, such as informational, veto power, or authorization—if I don't sign the check, we don't buy it—and all are worth delineating.

For completeness, we can specify five different buying roles applicable to both consumer and industrial product purchasing decisions:

1. Initiator.
2. Influencer.
3. Decider.
4. Purchaser.
5. User.

As indicated previously, the same person or different persons could potentially occupy each role. As a result, marketing managers must be aware of who occupies which role(s) and develop a promotional strategy accordingly.

Consumer Goods

The most obvious (and popular) basis for segmentation based on who is the customer is general characteristics. In the area of consumer goods, this usually means four general types of variables:

1. Demographic.   The most commonly used demographics are age, sex, geographic location, and stage in the life cycle. These characteristics have the advantage of being relatively easy to ascertain. Unfortunately, they are (with obvious exceptions such as baby food) generally only weakly related to behavior, and demographic-based segments are therefore often not very different in terms of behavior.

2. Socioeconomic.   Income and such related variables as education, occupation, and social class have been used as bases for segmentation with income and education generally being more useful. Again, as in the case of demographics, the relation between these variables and purchase behavior is fairly weak. In fact, for frequently purchased goods, demographics and socioeconomic variables typically account for less than 10 percent of the variation in purchase rates of a product category across households (Massy, Frank, & Wind, 1972; Massy, Frank, & Lodahl, 1968).

3. Personality.   Given the relatively limited predictive power of demographic and socioeconomic variables, the fact that many people in marketing are trained in psychology, and the natural desire to find a general basis for dividing up consumers that will be useful over many situations, it is not surprising that an attempt has been made to use personality traits as a basis for segmentation. Also not surprising, such traits as dominance and aggressiveness are typically not highly related to catsup consumption (see Kassarjian, 1971, for an extensive review of this area).

4. Psychographic.   Psychographics basically represent an evolution from general personality variables to attitudes and behaviors more closely related to consumption of goods and services. Psychographics, also known as lifestyle variables, generally fall into three categories: *A*ctivities (cooking, sports, and so on), *I*nterests (art, music), and *O*pinions. (Consequently, the description AIO.) These have been widely used as bases for segmentation by many companies (e.g., General Foods) and also have been used as the basis for the creation of advertising themes by ad agencies (e.g., Needham, Harper, and Steers). Recently, many researchers have begun using the VALS typology developed by SRI International as a basis for defining segments (Mitchell, 1983).

Industrial Goods
For industrial goods, by contrast, the use of personality or psychographic factors has been almost totally nonexistent. Here the focus has been on firm characteristics such as size of company, location, and sales, which are the logical equivalent of demographic and socioeconomic variables used for consumer products.

Probably the most widely used basis for industrial segmentation is the Standard Industrial Classification (SIC) coding system. This system, which is popular largely because of its availability, is maintained by the U.S. government as a basis for tracking output by industry. Two-digit codes indicate major industry groups (e.g., 34 is fabricated metal products), three digits indicate broadly defined industries (e.g., 344 is fabricated structural metal products), and four digits indicate fairly specific industries (e.g., 3442 is metal doors, sash frames, moldings, and trim). In spite of the problems in classifying multiproduct companies, this provides a useful basis for segmenting markets, especially for the purpose of assessing market potential (see Chapter 6).

What They Do

What the customers do falls into two basic groupings: what they purchase in the product category, and what they do with it. Concerning what they purchase within the product category, the two major variables are usage rate of the category and which *brands/products/services* are purchased. For many consumer goods, panel or similar data are available which contain purchase histories (e.g., brands purchased were A, A, A, B, A, A, C, A, A, A) on individual consumers. Such data can be analyzed by a variety of means to measure competitive patterns (e.g., percent of switching from A to B and vice versa).

For industrial and consumer goods, analysis of what (competing) product they currently use provides a useful basis for segmentation for new products. For example, a new plastic may be useful for replacing zinc, aluminum, brass, and so on. For Federal Express, this might consist of customers of Emery, Purolator, UPS, the U.S. Post Office, and so forth. Defining customers in terms of the product currently used can also lead to delineation of untapped customer segments.

Another way of looking at the "what" question is to see what they are doing with the product. One basic set of distinctions is:

1. Customer/final users.
2. Industrial customers, who incorporate your product in one or more products they make. These customers can be divided into those who manufacture and then try to sell the products and those who produce to specifications (e.g., contractors).
3. Resellers, who simply markup and resell your product, perhaps with a little packaging.

In addition, defining exactly what usage situation the product or service is used in is crucial to understanding customers. This includes both where they use it (e.g., at home or in the office) and how they actually employ it, which may or may not be related to why they originally bought it (e.g., a computer may have been bought to do payroll and end up acting as a word processor). Numerous examples exist of products being used in ways other than their original intent on the part of either seller or buyer or both. It is also useful to consider "how else" they might use it in order to uncover new market opportunities. This would also aid in determining possible generic competitors (see Chapter 2).

Where They Buy It

The location of purchase is a very important basis for segmentation. It falls into two major categories: where they seek information (that is, shop, which includes both stores and information sources such as magazines) and where they actually make the purchase (e.g., at home or the office, by mail, by two-way cable TV, and so on).

When They Buy

When they buy encompasses time of year, time of month, and even, potentially, time of day. Fast-food operators, for example, are known to segment by "daypart," that is, breakfast, lunch, dinner, and even "snacking" times. "When" can also include when they buy in terms of sales or price breaks and rebates on the assumption that those who buy on a deal may be different from those who pay full price.

Why They Buy

The most basic level of segmentation based on why they buy has to do with the basic need(s) the customer is attempting to satisfy (e.g., hunger). This level often defines the basic level of competition for the product. A more specific level of segmentation is possible in terms of the particular need the product or service is designed to serve. For example, a McDonald's meal may serve as a treat/reward for good performance by a kid, a meal to provide variety to a diet in the evening, or as a quick, convenient lunch. Similarly, a phone can serve as a means of "normal" communication, a status symbol, or a means to transmit data to a computer at another location.

The final level of the why question relates to specific attributes and features of the offer. These include at least seven categories:

1. Economic (e.g., price).
2. Performance.
3. Services offered by the seller (e.g., terms, training).
4. Source reliability (e.g., delivery).
5. Internal political (company policies, key influentials).
6. External political (legal constraints, pressure groups).
7. Psychological (personal tendencies, reference group behavior).

Notice that this can be applied to both the product category level decision (e.g., a computer) and the specific product or brand selected (e.g., a VAX 11-780). Notice also that the issue of why they buy is directly related to their responsiveness to changes in the product offering, which is a key basis for segmentation.

How They Buy It

An obvious means of describing customers is in terms of *how much* they buy, which allows a focus on the so-called heavy users. On another level, it is possible to separate customers based on *the way they buy* a product (e.g., cash versus on credit, direct versus through a middleman).

It is also useful to segment customers in terms of the procedure followed in making the selection. This includes not just the "rational" method in which specific benefits are considered but, more broadly, whether much deliberation is involved at all. Many purchases, though perhaps once based on careful consideration, are essentially *habitual* ("It's worked before, so...."), *indifference* ("They are all the same, so

.…"), or *trial* ("Looks like it's interesting, so.…") (O'Shaughnessy, 1984). Segmenting customers into the approach followed can provide useful insights into a market.

It is also useful to segment customers in terms of the procedure followed in extensive problem solving, limited problem solving, or routinized (Howard, 1977). In extensive problem solving (EPS), customers are concerned mainly with understanding how the product works, what it competes with, and how they would use it. EPS is generally found among first-time purchasers and products that are technologically new (e.g., 32-bit microprocessors, xerography). Limited problem solving occurs when the customer understands the basic functioning of the product and what it competes with and is concerned with evaluating the brand on a small number of attributes, typically in comparison to alternatives. This is generally the approach to most large-ticket purchases (e.g., a new piece of capital equipment). The third basic type of purchase is routinized. In this stage consumers essentially follow a predetermined rule for making decisions (e.g., "If we need a new typewriter, call IBM"; "If my car breaks down, call my friendly mechanic"; "If it's 10:30 break time, buy a Coke, unless Pepsi is 10 cents cheaper, in which case buy a Pepsi"). Most routine order purchases fall into this category, but so do many big ticket items. (I always buy a new appliance from my friendly GE dealer.) Since customers following this approach can be expected to ignore most information because they have already reached a decision (usually reinforced by satisfaction with past use), the implications for marketing strategy are dramatic. For a winning product bought routinely, make it easy for the customer to keep buying and advertise "The Real Thing" (Coke), "The System Is the Solution" (AT&T), and so forth. If your product doesn't have much market share and you want to increase it, then you must "shock" the customer into considering your product either by urging variety seeking "The Uncola" (7UP), or by promotions or price breaks, the ultimate of which is a free sample.

Another related way to monitor how it is bought is to consider where the product is in its product life cycle. New products are generally first purchased through specialty outlets, but as the products become better known they tend to be more often purchased through mass merchandisers. Put bluntly, eventually everything will be sold by K mart.

Another useful distinction in how they buy is between (*a*) planned, (*b*) routine, (*c*) impulse, and (*d*) emergency purchases. One would expect a different buying process in the case of an emergency replacement, whether it be a toilet bowl seat in a house or a generator in a manufacturing plant. In fact, keeping track of the fraction of purchases of each type is a very useful analysis in many circumstances.

Finally, when multiple decision makers are involved, deciding how they reach consensus (e.g., unanimity—everyone has a veto; democracy—everyone is equal; dictatorship—one person is the key; or turn-taking) is a useful way to gain insight into the customer.

SEGMENTATION

Assuming we have described customers as based in Figure 5–1, it is now appropriate to group the customers into segments. (Of course, if there are only five customers, no grouping is required since we can treat each one separately.)

Selecting a Basis for Segmentation

Given the tremendous number of potential bases for segmentation, the pertinent question that arises is: Which one to use? Actually several can be used in combination, so the question is really: What makes a basis for segmentation a good one? This is especially crucial since analysis (e.g., heavy users care more about price). While there is no single way to say what is best (anyone suggesting there is probably doesn't understand the problem), the following five criteria provide a useful standard for evaluation:

1. Sizable.   Segments must be of sufficient size in terms of potential sales (but not in terms of number of customers) to be worth worrying about. (As a rule billion dollar companies don't care much about J. R. Smith at 1188 Maple Street, or all the people on Maple Street for that matter.)

2. Identifiable.   Segments should be identifiable so that when presenting results they can be referred to by more pleasing titles than Segment A, Segment B (e.g., the 35 to 50 segment, the sports-minded, companies in New York).

3. Reachable.   It may be sufficient for strategic purposes to identify a segment. For purposes of planning the marketing mix (e.g., advertising), however, it is useful to be able to target efforts on a segment.

Therefore, a sports-minded segment tends to be reachable through the media (e.g., *Sports Illustrated*), whereas people who prefer the color blue, though identified, may be too hard to reach (except by labels on blue towels, or by copy that employs the color blue).

4. Respond Differently. Ideally, segments should respond differently to at least some of the elements of the offering. If all segments respond the same, then no specialized programs can be used. For example, some customers may be sensitive to advertising but not price, whereas others are concerned about price but unaffected by advertising, and still others care about a single attribute such as downtime. The sensitivity to changes in market offering forms a useful basis for both describing the overall market and defining segments. It also makes the "why they buy" part of the analysis particularly crucial.

5. Stable. Since future plans are based on past data, segments (and hopefully but not necessarily the members of those segments) should be fairly stable over time.

Methods for deriving segments:
1. Databased.
   a. General characteristics.
      One way of generating segments is to collect data from a sample of customers on a series of variables and then form groups by means of cluster analysis. This is sometimes called looking for natural clusters, which was the purpose of cluster analysis in fields such as biology. When one sees the mathematics involved, however, it is clear that the process is anything but natural. Nonetheless, this method produces clusters that are sometimes quite interesting. One example of this is the lifestyle-based clusters used by advertising agencies in designing copy strategy.
      Another example involves grouping consumers of soft drinks based on their purchase frequencies of eight soft drinks (Bass, Pessemier, & Lehmann, 1972; Lehmann, 1976). Here 10 segments were formed (Table 5-1) providing an interesting view of the market in terms of brand preference, with a segment emerging as loyal to each of the three largest-selling brands: Coke, Pepsi, and 7UP.
   b. Criterion-related segmentation.
      Rather than treat all the variables available as "equals" as in cluster analysis, this method assumes one variable is the criterion

TABLE 5–1
Average Purchase Probability by Brand

Segment	Percentage of Sample	Coke	7UP	Tab	Like	Pepsi	Sprite	Diet Pepsi	Fresca
1	14.0	.58	.04	.02	.06	.15	.07	.02	.07
2	13.2	.91	.03	.01	.01	.02	.01	.00	.01
3	16.5	.17	.11	.02	.04	.52	.06	.02	.06
4	10.3	.06	.74	.01	.03	.03	.10	.01	.02
5	3.7	.07	.11	.00	.01	.10	.64	.00	.06
6	6.6	.08	.04	.11	.16	.12	.02	.40	.07
7	8.6	.10	.25	.08	.16	.08	.17	.05	.11
8	11.9	.06	.03	.00	.00	.86	.04	.00	.01
9	11.1	.40	.30	.02	.04	.11	.07	.01	.05
10	4.1	.11	.06	.04	.09	.10	.10	.02	.48

Source: Donald R. Lehmann, "An Empirically Based Stochastic Model," *Journal of Business Research* 4, no. 4 (November 1976), p. 352.

(e.g., product class usage) and then attempts to find which other variables (e.g., age, income) are most highly related to it. The market is then segmented on the basis of these variables.

A variety of statistical procedures are available for such studies, including cross-tabulation, analysis of variance, and AID (see Table 5–2, a list of analytical methods examining customer differences). At least for the first stages of such research, however, some form of regression analysis is frequently used. In performing such regressions it is often useful to treat the variables as "categorical" (by using a series of so-called dummy variables). In any event, these regressions (at least for frequently purchased consumer products) tend to produce poor fits with individual behavior. Yet, in spite of the low Rs, these regressions often point to useful bases for segmentation. For example, Bass, Tigert, and Lonsdale (1968) found significant differences in product category usage based on demographics such as age and income (Table 5–3). Similar results were found by Assael and Roscoe (1976) in segmenting the market of long-distance phone expenditures.

2. A priori.

There is a strong tendency to want to derive segments by examining data. Still, some of the most useful segmentation studies are based on such simple bases as customer lists (heavy users, light users, non-

TABLE 5–2
Analytical Methods for Examining Customer Differences

Identifying relations among two variables:
  Cross-tabs (categorical variables)
  Correlations (continuous variables)
Predicting a criterion variable based on several other variables:
  ANOVA
  Regression
  Discriminant analysis
  AID (Automatic Interaction Detector)
Simplifying a database:
  Factor analysis: identifying redundant variables
  Cluster analysis: forming segments
  Multidimensional scaling: Graphically representing a number of alternatives on a
    small number of dimensions

users). While these are not elegant, they are often more useful than so-called natural clusters because they are readily identifiable and reachable and obviously have responded differently to the product offering. In fact, it is always advisable to use such segmentation strategy as at least a basis for comparison with the results of more "data massaging"–oriented approaches.

No simple way exists to tell how to get the best segmentation scheme. In that respect it's a lot like art—you can tell whether you like it or not but never prove it's the best. Nonetheless, a final product should be readily usable, as Figure 5–2 shows.

CUSTOMER VALUE

Having described various bases for customer analysis, it should be clear that many of the bases related to how much the product is worth to the customer or why the customer buys and uses the product service. The assessment of this worth, often known as customer value, is so basic to not only segmentation but to strategy in general, that this section goes into the topic in some depth.

Definition. Customer value is the net benefit to a consumer of obtaining a particular product/brand/service.

More specifically, customer value can be considered to be composed of three basic elements.

TABLE 5–3
Light and Heavy Buyers by Mean Purchase Rates for Different Socioeconomic Cells

R^2	Product	Description Light Buyers	Description Heavy Buyers	Mean Consumption Rate Ranges Light Buyers	Mean Consumption Rate Ranges Heavy Buyers	Ratio of Highest to Lowest Rate
.08	Catsup	Unmarried or married over age 50 without children	Under 50, three or more children	.74–1.82	2.73–5.79	7.8
.07	Frozen orange juice	Under 35 or over 65, income less than $10,000, not college grads, two or less children	College grads, income over $10,000, between 35 and 65	1.12–2.24	3.53–9.00	8.0
.04	Pancake mix	Some college, two or less children	Three or more children, high school or less education	.48–.52	1.10–1.51	3.3
.08	Candy bars	Under 35, no children	35 or over, three or more children	1.01–4.31	6.56–22.29	21.9
	Cake mix	Not married or under 35, no children, income under $10,000, TV less than 3½ hours	35 or over, three or more children, income over $10,000	.55–1.10	2.22–3.80	6.9
.09	Beer	Under 25 or over 50, college education, nonprofessional, TV less than 2 hours	Between 25 and 50, not college graduate, TV more than 3½ hours	0–12.33	17.26–40.30	—
.02	Cream shampoo	Income less than $8,000, at least some college, less than five children	Income $10,000 or over with high school or less education	16–35	44–87	5.5
.06	Hair spray	Over 65, under $8,000 income	Under 65, over $10,000 income, not college graduate	0–.41	.52–1.68	—
.09	Toothpaste	Over 50, less than three children, income less than $8,000	Under 50, three or more children, over $10,000 income	1.41–2.01	2.22–4.39	3.1
.03	Mouthwash	Under 35 or over 65, less than $8,000 income, some college	Between 35 and 65, income over $8,000, high school or less education	.46–.85	.98–1.17	2.5

Source: Frank Bass, Douglas Tigert, and Ronald Lonsdale, "Market Segmentation—Group versus Individual Behavior," Reprinted from *Journal of Marketing Research*, published by the American Marketing Association 5 (August 1968), p. 267.

FIGURE 5–2
Segmentation of Ski Buyers

Segment	Hero	Basic Values	Resorts	Skis and Boots	Clothing	Product	Price	Distribution	Advertising
Social skiers	Suzy Chaffee	Looking good, fresh air	Convenient, intermediate (Stratton, Bromley)	Look good, easy to use	Matching outfits	Package deals	Anything reasonable	One-stop shopping, convenient, ski shops	Social
Hot non-experts	James Bond, downhill racer	Being seen, adrenalin rush	Good lift lines, sufficient challenge (Hunter, Mount Snow)	Just below top of the line	Stylishly outlandish	Popular models	Moderate	Malls, Herman's	Self-image
Serious exercisers	Grizzly Adams	Work out, being outdoors	Challenge and variety (Pico, Burke)	Value for the money, good to top of the line	Comfort, last year's/decade's style	Performance, versatility	Price conscious	Sales, discounters	Informational
Performance seekers	Ingemar Stenmark	Being tested, improving	Big and steep, moguls (Stowe, Mad River)	Top of the line	Comfort, functional	Special characteristics	Will pay for quality	Willing to seek out	Informational

1. Importance of the usage situation.
2. Effectiveness of the product category in the situation.
3. Effectiveness of the brand in the situation.

Notice that there are two basic notions of value: *absolute* value which essentially assumes that no competing products exist, and *relative* value which is the value to the consumer given the existence of all other products. Relative, not absolute, customer value is the key to decision making by both customers and companies. Thus, to be of greatest value, a product has to be the best in a product class, be in a product class which is best suited to a usage situation, and be directed toward an important usage situation.

MANIFESTATIONS

While all products presumably have some value, a variety of signs of the value of a product are evident even without special efforts to measure them. The value of the product also includes the following factors.

1. *Price.*   Price is the company's assessment of the product's value.
2. *Price sensitivity.*   A product whose sales stay constant when prices increase generally is of greater value than the price.
3. *Complaints and compliments.*   The number of complaints and/ or compliments received by the company gives an indication of the product's value.
4. *Word of mouth.*   Although hard to measure, word of mouth comments provide a useful subjective assessment of a product's value.
5. *Margin/profit contribution.*   Generally higher margins indicate semimonopoly positions and, therefore, higher relative value.
6. *Dollar sales.*   Total dollar sales provide an aggregate measure of the value of a product as assessed by the market.
7. *Competitive activity.*   Competitive activity such as new product introductions indicates that the total gap between customer value and company costs is sufficiently large to allow for profits even when more companies divide the difference.
8. *Repeat purchase rate.*   High loyalty indicates high brand value.

A METHOD FOR ASSESSING THE VALUE OF THE PRODUCT CATEGORY

Many ways can be devised to estimate the value of a product category. The method presented here requires four steps:

1. *Determining the uses.*   Determine the present and potential uses to which a particular product category may be put (see the Chapter 2 discussion on determining generic competitors). This is usually done by a combination of "logical analysis" (e.g., asking people involved with the product or a "creative" individual what the product can do) plus customer data in the form of surveys of present users or focus groups.

2. *Estimating the importance of the uses.*   In addition to introspection, survey methods that either directly ask the importance question ("On a scale of X to Y, how important are the following?") or attempt to get at importance indirectly (e.g., "If a user of this product found that it failed to operate properly, how badly would he be affected?") are often used. Another useful measure of importance is the total sales potential of products which serve this use.

3. *Listing the competing product categories.*   The present and potential categories that service each of the uses. Determination of competitive products, described in greater detail elsewhere in this book, can be based on published sources, sales records, salespeople, introspection, or surveys which ask questions such as "How appropriate/useful is X as a replacement for Y?"

4. *Determining the relative effectiveness of the product category in each usage situation.*   Besides introspection and expert opinion, a survey can address this by asking either, "How effective is X?" or "How much better is X than Y?"

The value of the product category (*VPC*) is then indicated by the sum over all uses of the importance of the use times the relative effectiveness of the product category:

$$VPC = \sum_{\text{all uses}} (\text{Importance}) \times (\text{Relative effectiveness})$$

More important than the total *VPC,* however, is the relative effectiveness of the product category for each usage situation, since these generally define market segments.

An example of this approach, based on the microcomputer industry, appears as Table 5–4. Rather than using numbers on some scales (e.g.,

TABLE 5–4
Microcomputer Product Category Value Estimation (Random Customer #007)

Use	(IMP) Importance	Competitive Products	(REL) Relative Effectiveness	(IMP) × (REL)
Video games	Some 20	TV attachments, board games	Very good	High
Bookkeeping	None 1	Accountant, service bureau, "books"	Marginal	Low
Learning skills	Very low 4	Books, school	Inferior	Low
Data analysis	Large 65	Large-scale computer, time sharing, consultant, calculator	Good	High
Report preparation	A little 10	Typewriter, word processor, secretarial service	OK	Fairly low
	$\overline{100}$			

rating relative effectiveness from 1 to 10), this example used adjectives. A numerical system is better, but only after the analysis is performed on enough product categories to know which numbers are good/big and which are not. From Table 5–4 it should be noted that (*a*) it is fairly easy to structure the table, (*b*) some of the entries will be hard to quantify, and (*c*) limited confidence is likely to exist in many of the entries. The difficulty in quantifying the entries is a problem if one desires a precise estimate of the value. Still, even such entries as "not very effective" can provide guidance as to the product's value. Regarding the limited confidence in some of the entries, the appropriate procedure is to vary each of the entries and see if it matters. If the value is sensitive to relatively small variations, this suggests an area where more precise research is needed.

Assessing the Value of the Brand/Product Service

Assessing the total value of a brand can be done indirectly. A high value brand has:

1. High share.
2. High repeat purchase rate.
3. Low elasticity with respect to price, and so on.
4. Limited competitive brand shopping.

Using customer responses to estimate the value of a product generally involves direct ratings of the brand. This includes three basic approaches:

1. *Direct ratings* on a scale (e.g., "How good is *X* for use *Y*?") for all competing products and then a comparison. (Remember we are generally interested in relative and not absolute value. Therefore, an average of 4 on a 5-point scale indicates good values if the other products are getting 2s and 3s, but little value if the other products are getting averages of 4.5 and 4.8).

2. *Constant sum ratings across brands,* such as "Please rate the following four brands in terms of how well they work in use by dividing 10 points among them:"

Brand A _____
Brand B _____
Brand C _____
Brand D _____
　　　　　_____
　　　10

3. *Graded paired comparisons* requires customers to indicate which of a pair of products is preferred and by how much. This is often done in terms of dollar amounts (Pessemier, 1963), as shown in Table 5–5.

Components of Value

While knowing the total value of a brand is useful for both entry/exit and pricing decisions, understanding the components of the product which produce its value is also important. The idea that a product is a bundle of characteristics and that each characteristic has value is widely recognized (Fishbein, 1967; Lancaster, 1966; Rosenberg, 1956). Essen-

TABLE 5–5
Dollar Metric Example: Soft Drink Preference

Data

Pair of Brands (more preferred brand circled)	Amount Extra Willing to Pay to Get a Six Pack of the More Preferred Brand (cents)
(Coke,) Pepsi	2
(Coke,) 7UP	8
(Coke,) Dr Pepper	5
(Coke,) Fresca	12
(Pepsi,) 7UP	6
(Pepsi,) Dr Pepper	3
(Pepsi,) Fresca	10
7UP, (Dr Pepper)	3
(7UP,) Fresca	4
(Dr Pepper,) Fresca	7

Analysis

Coke:	+2 (versus Pepsi) + 8 (versus 7UP) + 5 (versus Dr Pepper) + 12 (versus Fresca)	=	27
Pepsi:	−2 + 6 + 3 + 10	=	17
7UP:	−8 − 6 − 3 + 4	=	−13
Dr Pepper:	−5 − 3 + 3 + 7	=	2
Fresca:	−12 − 10 − 4 − 7	=	−33

tially, this suggests that the value of each product is the sum of its values on the characteristics that make it up:

Product value $= \sum$ (Value of positions on the characteristics)

The characteristics, as mentioned earlier, fall into seven major categories: economic, performance, source service, sources reliability, internal political, external political, and psychological. In order to operationalize this approach, three major steps are needed.

Identify Important Characteristics

Expert Opinion. In a well-established product category this is likely to be very useful.

Survey Data. This is generally best done by direct ratings (e.g., "How important is X?"). Importance ratings generally have two problems: Everything tends to be rated as important (and, therefore, relative importance is the key), and certain socially desirable answers are given (nutrition is important, and so on). Often key dimensions can be uncovered by indirect methods such as multidimensional scaling of similarity ratings (which the subject can produce without exposing his or her "biases") or by the less elegant but effective tool of focus groups.

Analysis of Buying Patterns. One measure of the importance of a characteristic is customers' resistance to giving it up. Therefore, characteristics a customer does not switch on (e.g., diet versus nondiet soft drinks) are considered important.

Position on Characteristics

Expert Opinion. These are useful but often wrong, since they tend to be based on engineering specifications rather than customer perceptions.

Survey Data. Both direct ratings ("How much of characteristic X does Product Y have?") and similarity-based positionings derived via multidimensional scaling are used.

Purchase Behavior. By examining switching across products, it is possible to create a geometric model in which pairs of brands among which there is substantial switching are close together, and those pairs among which there is little switching are far apart. The identity of the dimensions of this space are interpreted as the key characteristics.

Evaluation of the Value of the Positions

For many characteristics more is better, so by simply multiplying an importance measure times the amount of the characteristic, the value can be ascertained [e.g., Product value = Σ (Importance of characteristic) (Amount of characteristic)]. When such a linear relationship does not hold, it is possible to either consider the value in relation to desired levels on the characteristics [e.g., Product value = Σ (Importance of characteristics) (Difference between the actual and the desired level of the product)]. When characteristics are essentially discrete (e.g., colors, dinner entrées), each value must be estimated separately. The most common approach in such situations is some form of trade-off or conjoint analysis.

This section has attempted to describe customer value—what it is and how it is measured. A summary of the approach appears in Figure 5–3. Assessing customer value is difficult but crucial. Complicating factors include the multiple uses for products and the fact that different people value different characteristics differently, which argues for analysis by segments. Still, if a firm can actually gauge relative customer value of a product, which is the unique ability of a product to satisfy needs, it can plan much more effectively either how to market the existing product efficiently or how to create a new product that will be highly valued by

FIGURE 5–3
Assessing Customer Value

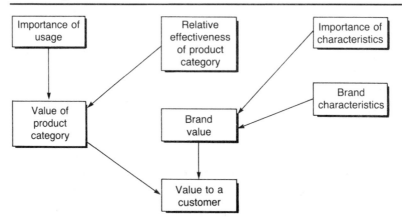

the market. Also, the greater the relative customer value, the greater the "monopoly" power of the firm and, therefore, the greater both the profits that can accrue to the firm and the satisfaction that can be gained by the customer.

SUMMARY

Assuming a customer analysis has been completed, a summary in the form of Figure 5–4 can be compiled. Using Diet Pepsi, for example, the segments might be teenagers, fast-food chains, and so on. Notice that these can overlap, as teenagers are the customers of the fast-food chains, but distinguishing between fountain and supermarket sales is probably worth doing. For Federal Express, the segments are likely to be formed on the basis of type of company (e.g., law firm).

In analyzing the customer, it is only natural to look at history. Nonetheless, the reason for doing so is not to be a good historian, but to be a good forecaster. Put differently, one needs to make judgments about what might cause behavior to change (both your actions and those out-

FIGURE 5–4
Basic Format for Summarizing Customer Analysis

Customer Description	Segment				
	I	*II*	*III*	*IV*	. . .
Who they are					
What they do					
Where they buy					
When they buy					
Why they buy					
How they buy					
How many there are (segment size)					
How fast they are growing					
Customer value of product category					
Customer value of brand					

side influences: culture, competition, economic regulation, and so on). In addition, some assessment is needed of the likelihood these "causal" influences will in fact change. Finally, analysis of the impact of the likely or reasonable changes on customer behavior, and consequently sales, must be completed. Then and only then will customer analysis be useful for deciding on what you will do in the future and what trends you will monitor most closely.

REFERENCES

Assael, Henry, and A. Marvin Roscoe, Jr. "Approaches to Market Segmentation Analysis." *Journal of Marketing* 40 (October 1976), pp. 67–76.

Bass, Frank M.; Edgar A. Pessemier; and Donald R. Lehmann. "An Experimental Study of Relationship between Attitudes, Brand Preference, and Choice." *Behavioral Science* 17 (November 1972), pp. 532–41.

Bass, Frank M.; Douglas J. Tigert, Jr.; and Ronald T. Lonsdale. "Market Segmentation—Group versus Individual Behavior." *Journal of Marketing Research* 5, no. 3 (August 1968), pp. 264–70.

Belk, Russell W. "Situational Variables and Consumer Behavior." *The Journal of Consumer Research* 2, no. 3 (December 1975), pp. 157–64.

Cravens, David W.; Gerald E. Hills; and Robert B. Woodruff. *Marketing Decision Making: Concepts and Strategy.* Rev. ed. Homewood, Ill.: Richard D. Irwin, 1980.

Doyle, Peter, and John Saunders. "Market Segmentation and Positioning in Specialized Industrial Markets." *Journal of Marketing* 49 (Spring 1985), pp. 24–32.

Ferber, Robert, ed. *Handbook of Marketing Research.* New York: McGraw-Hill, 1974.

Fishbein, Martin. "Attitudes and the Prediction of Behavior." In *Readings in Attitude Theory and Measurement,* ed. Martin Fishbein. New York: John Wiley & Sons, 1967, pp. 477–92.

Frank, Ronald E.; William F. Massy; and Yoram Wind. *Market Segmentation.* New York: Prentice-Hall, 1972.

Green, Paul E., and Wayne S. DeSarbo. "Componential Segmentation in the Analysis of Consumer Trade-Offs." *Journal of Marketing* 43 (Fall 1979), pp. 83–91.

Howard, John A. *Consumer Behavior: Application of Theory.* New York: McGraw-Hill, 1977.

"The IBM-DEC Wars: It's 'The Year of the Customer.'" *Business Week,* March 30, 1987, pp. 86–87.

Kassarjian, Harold H. "Personality and Consumer Behavior: A Review." *Journal of Marketing Research* 8, no. 4 (November 1971), pp. 409–19.

Kotler, Philip. *Marketing Management: Analysis, Planning, and Control.* 4th ed. Englewood Cliffs, N.J.: Prentice-Hall, 1980.

Lancaster, Kelvin J. "A New Approach to Consumer Theory." *Journal of Political Economy* 74 (April 1966), pp. 132–57.

Lehmann, Donald R. "An Empirically Based Stochastic Model." *Journal of Business Research* 4, no. 4 (November 1976), pp. 347–56.

Massy, William F.; Ronald E. Frank; and Thomas M. Lodahl. *Purchasing Behavior and Personal Attributes.* Philadelphia: University of Pennsylvania Press, 1968.

Mitchell, Arnold. *The Nine American Life Styles.* New York: Warner Books, 1983.

O'Shaughnessy, John. *Competitive Marketing: A Strategic Approach.* Winchester, Mass.: Allen & Unwin, 1984.

Pessemier, Edgar A. *Experimental Methods of Analyzing Demand for Branded Consumer Goods with Applications to Problems in Marketing Strategy.* Bulletin No. 39. Pullman: Washington State University, Bureau of Economic and Business Research, June 1963.

Rosenberg, M. J. "Cognitive Structure and Attitudinal Affect." *Journal of Abnormal and Social Psychology* 53 (November 1956), pp. 367–72.

Warshaw, Paul R. "A New Model for Predicting Behavioral Intentions: An Alternative to Fishbein." *Journal of Marketing Research* 17 (May 1980), pp. 153–72.

Wells, William D. "Psychographics: A Critical Review." *Journal of Marketing Research* 12 (May 1975), pp. 196–213.

Winter, Frederick W. "A Cost-Benefit Approach to Market Segmentation." *Journal of Marketing* 43 (Fall 1979), pp. 103–11.

CHAPTER 6

MARKET POTENTIAL AND FORECASTING

OVERVIEW

In order to make intelligent decisions regarding which strategy to follow and what level of activity to plan for, it is important to try to estimate the results (typically in terms of sales in units) of various courses of action. This, in turn, requires knowing what might happen (potential) and what we think will happen (forecast). This chapter deals with the development of potential estimates and forecasts. Since the potentials are often an input to a forecast, we discuss these first.

Definitions

The terms *potential, forecast,* and *quota* are used in many contexts. For purposes of this book, we will adopt the following definitions:

Potential: The maximum reasonably attainable under a given set of conditions (or, in older English, what "thou" might achieve). Put differently, sales under essentially 100 percent distribution and heavy advertising and promotion.

Forecast: That which you expect to achieve under a given set of conditions (what "thou" should achieve).

Quota: That which you are expected to achieve (what "thou" best achieve).

These definitions suggest several points:

1. Potentials and forecasts exist at both the industry/market or firm level.

	Expectations	*Possibilities*
Firm	Sales forecast	Sales potential
Industry	Market forecast	Market potential

Since our focus is on firm level planning, we will focus on the sales forecast and discuss market forecasts and market potentials as means to reach the sales forecast.

2. Both potentials and forecasts depend on a set of conditions. These conditions can be divided into four major categories: (*a*) what customers do, (*b*) what the firm does, (*c*) what competitors do, and (*d*) what occurs in the general environment (economy, culture).

3. Potentials and forecasts are time dependent. Stated differently, what may not be possible in the short run (e.g., 1 year) may be quite attainable in the longer term (e.g., 10 years). While strategic plans depend on long-term potentials, annual plans focus primarily on short-run potentials and forecasts.

As an aside, this suggests a trap into which a firm can fall. By optimizing short-run decisions, the firm may be making what in the long run is a less than optimal series of decisions. It is for that reason that products often are assigned different objectives, such as increasing sales (when the long-term potential seems large and increasing) or maximizing cash flow (when the long-term potential appears low).

4. Quotas are essentially required levels of performance. While these ideally should be flexible as conditions warrant, they are typically treated as "nonnegotiable" demands.

Why They Are Used

The major uses of potential estimates are essentially threefold:

1. To Make Entry/Exit Decisions. Potentials (both market and sales) are the key numbers in the strategic decisions of what markets to be in.

2. To Make Location Decisions. Both manufacturing plants and distribution facilities tend to be located based on potential estimates as do retail stores.

3. As an Input to Forecasts. The major use of potentials in annual planning is as a basis for the sales forecast. This suggests that the forecast can be viewed as the product of potential times the percent of potential expected to be achieved.

The major uses of forecasts are discussed in detail at this point.

1. To Answer "What If" Questions.   In considering which strategy and tactics to follow, the key information is an estimate of the outcomes of the various strategies and tactics, typically the sales and profit levels. The simplest "what if" question is what will happen next year if everything remains as it has been in the past, which makes the forecast basically an extrapolation.

2. To Set Budgets.   Sales forecasts become the basis of a budget since they specify both sales level to be attained and, by implication, the resources needed. All pro forma income statements use a sales forecast as their basis.

3. To Establish a Basis for a Monitoring System.   Deviations from forecasts serve as a warning to management to reexamine a market and their strategy in it. For example, assume we had market potential estimates and sales data for several regions (Figure 6–1). In this case, the relation between potential and actual sales is quite close. Therefore, the sales-versus-potential curve could be used for evaluating performance. Those regions whose sales fall above the upper control limit would be classified as "good," while those whose sales fall below the lower control limit would be "bad." While these results could then be tied directly to compensation for regional managers, this might not be appropriate. For example, a region that did very well could have done so because an important competitor folded or a major promotion was staged. Similarly, a region that did badly could have done so because of at least five reasons:

1. Increased competitive pressure.
2. Potential was overestimated (e.g., Soft-Batch cookies).
3. Nonoptimal strategy determination and/or execution.
4. Capacity limitations.
5. Inadequate effort by the industry as a whole.

Consequently, the best use of forecasts (or market potential estimates) for control is as a warning device to indicate when a region is doing especially well or poorly. One should then attempt to determine why (good management, competition, luck, and so on) the region had an exceptional performance and learn something from it.

FIGURE 6–1
Hypothetical Sales versus Market Potential Data

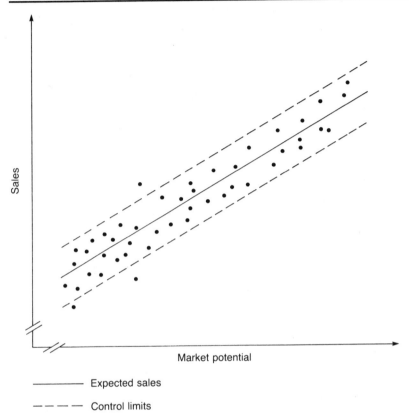

By contrast, quotas are used to establish goals. When there are sales goals, for example, they indicate to regional managers and salespeople what they are expected to achieve. Also sales goals establish standards for performance evaluation, typically at a very disaggregated (e.g., salesperson) level.

What Must Be Forecast

This chapter treats the sales forecast as the most crucial estimate. Thus, potentials serve mainly as an input to forecasts, and quotas are essentially an apportioning of the forecast to various subunits of the organization. Sales forecasts then become the basis for pro forma income (profit and loss) statements, which become the summary of the impact of the budget in the plan as well as the basis for selecting among several strategies.

As mentioned earlier, a good forecast takes into account four major categories of variables: customer behavior, company actions, competitive actions, and the environment. Company actions are assumed to be predictable; although in companies not organized around a product management concept many decisions, such as advertising and pricing, may be made in a piecemeal rather than an integrated fashion. By contrast, customer and competitive actions are much harder to forecast. In any event, the forecasts of customer and competitive actions are those which come out of the customer and competitive analysis parts of the plan. The general environment consists of such elements as state of the economy, key industries in it, demographic changes in the population, and costs of basic resources. While these elements can be forecast by the company, they are generally derived from secondary sources, such as government projections, and appear in the situation analysis as part of the industry analysis and/or the planning assumptions section of the plan. While environmental changes affect the plan mainly through their impact on customer and competitive behavior, they are so crucial that they are treated separately here.

The forecasting phase of the planning process ideally can be thought of as the process of assessing the possible outcome under all "reasonably" likely combinations of the four basic determinants of outcome. Notice, however, this suggests that achieving forecasts only by varying company decisions without considering competitive reactions is, unless the competitors are asleep, insufficient. The forecasting process can be viewed as a process of filling out a three-dimensional grid (Figure 6–2) with the likely outcomes.

It is useful to emphasize that the forecast in each cell should not be a single number but a range of possible outcomes. Thus, while a forecast of 21,274.43 parts may sound better than 21,000 ± 4,000, it may only be misleading and an example of foolish precision. Put differently, do not expect forecasts to six decimal places, especially when such precision is not crucial to making a sound decision.

While a "best guess" forecast is useful, so is data on the upper and lower bounds on the outcome. Knowing the range of likely results is crucial for strategy selection. A firm may be unwilling to undertake a strategy with a high expected result (e.g., a profit of $8 million) but which also has a reasonably likely disastrous result (e.g., loss of $5 million). Conversely, a firm may be willing to gamble on a possible large

FIGURE 6–2
Format for Forecasts

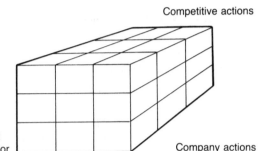

Competitive actions

General environment
and customer behavior

Company actions

return (e.g., a profit of $20,000) even if the likely result is a small profit or even a loss. It is also useful to know the likely range of outcomes for purposes of monitoring and control. For example, a drop of 30 percent below the forecast may be well within the expected range and therefore not necessarily cause for a major reanalysis in one situation, whereas in a different situation a 15 percent drop below the forecast may signal a serious problem.

At this point, it should be clear that to produce a forecast for each possible combination is a tedious task at best. Consequently, it is desirable to limit the task to, say, three environments (expected, benign, and hostile) and a limited number of competitive postures (e.g., status quo, more aggressive). This limitation should, however, be made with two points in mind. First, the initial forecasts may suggest a promising avenue or potential disaster that may lead to refining the scenarios. Second, it is important to recognize that the assumptions made here are crucial; therefore it is desirable to designate them formally as "planning assumptions."

Level of Accuracy Needed

Obviously, more accuracy in a forecast is better than less. Also, assuming a reasonably intelligent forecasting procedure is being employed (something one should *not* generally assume), then the only way to get a better forecast is to spend more time, effort, and money. Since increasing forecast accuracy has severely diminishing marginal returns (to make the range of a forecast half as large will generally at least quadruple the cost of a forecast), at some point the cost of improving the forecast will exceed the benefit.

The benefit of a better forecast usually is greater when (*a*) the price of the product being forecast is high in either absolute or relative terms ($10,000 may not seem much to IBM but it sure does to me); (*b*) the product demand is relatively volatile; and (*c*) the cost of an error in forecasting (including reorder cost and the cost of being out of stock—which may include the long-term loss of a disenchanted customer) is high. The cost of a better forecast increases as (*a*) the number of items or product forms increases (e.g., machine tool A with feature X, with features X and Z, and so on); (*b*) the forecasting method becomes more complicated to use; and (*c*) the forecast (and its basis) is difficult to communicate to others in the organization. (Generally speaking, review committees prefer not to hear about Fourier series, correlated errors, and so on).

ESTIMATING MARKET AND SALES POTENTIAL: BASICS

Market potential may be estimated in a variety of ways. Clearly, the details involved will depend heavily on the particular industry and product under consideration. What this section does is to suggest some general approaches to assessing potential.

Figure 6–3 summarizes a general process for deriving potential estimates (which is useful for forecast development as well). The exact data collected and calculations used depend on the type of situation encountered. Nonetheless, some general categories of data exist.

Before spending too much time developing one's own potential estimates, it is advisable to consult the available sources as discussed here.

1. *Government sources.* Market size estimates are available for many industries from sources such as the U.S. Department of Commerce and the Bureau of the Census (e.g., *Survey of Current Business, Current Industrial Reports*). Even when specific forecasts for the industry or product a person is interested in are not available, government data may be useful as input to his or her potential estimate. Examples include breakdowns of industry by location, size, and Standard Industrial Classification (SIC) code, and forecasts of general economic conditions.

2. *Trade associations.* Another free source of information.

FIGURE 6–3
Deriving Potential Estimates

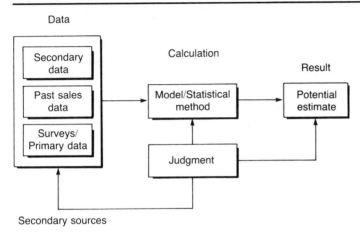

3. *Private companies.* A number of private companies track and forecast sales for various industries (e.g., Find/SVP, Predicasts, Morton). Some also survey capital spending plans (e.g., McGraw-Hill) and consumer sentiment and plans (e.g., Survey Research Center at the University of Michigan).
4. *Financial analysts.* Industry specialists often provide forecasts and/or potential estimates for various industries (e.g., Gartner Group for computers). Some of this material finds its way into the popular press (e.g., *Fortune, Forbes, Business Week*).

Past Sales

Clearly, past sales data are useful to have; however, in new markets they may be unavailable, inaccurate, or unduly influenced by isolated events. Therefore, just because such data are available does *not* mean other data should be ignored.

Primary Data/Surveys

Primary databased potential numbers begin to straddle the line between potentials and forecasts. Since, for example, surveys typically ask "What will you do?" or "If X occurs, what will you do?" they are mainly forecast oriented. So, rather than discuss the survey approach in detail here, we defer that discussion to the section "Sales Forecasting Methods."

Assessing the Value of a New or Growing Product: Initial Purchase

In considering both the saturation level (ultimate potential) and the time pattern of development, it is useful to consider the product vis-à-vis its major (and presumably older) competitor. This can be accomplished by considering three major dimensions.

1. Relative Advantage.   In terms of benefits provided, is the newer product superior in all respects and by what amount? Noticeably superior benefits will increase both the saturation level and the rate at which the level is achieved. Also, in general, relative advantage of the new product will increase over time as various modifications and line extensions appear.

2. Risk.   The greater the risk involved (financial, possible impact on product quality if a new component fails, and so on), the lower the probability that someone will buy the new product. Typically, risk—at least in terms of price—tends to drop over time, thus increasing the saturation level.

3. Compatibility.   The fewer and less major the changes required to adopt the new product, the faster it will be adopted. It is important to note that compatibility issues relate not only to the customers but to middlemen, the company itself (e.g., sales staff), and, if the customer uses a certain product or component in a product, their customer as well. Therefore, if a chemical company is planning to manufacture a new product, issues of manufacturing compatibility and sales staff effort arise within the company along with the behavior of wholesalers (assuming the product is sold through that channel), customer problems (Is retooling required?), and eventual customer acceptance (e.g., it took a long time to convince customers that plastic parts were acceptable in automobiles, even when both molders and the auto manufacturers were convinced). Again, as in the case of risk, incompatibility tends to decrease over time. Finally, incompatibility may be primarily psychological (i.e., "We just don't do things that way here."), and failure to consider the psychological barriers to adoption is often disastrous, at least in assessing a short-term potential.

Role of Analogous Products

Examining the pattern of use and adoption of analogous products or services is often quite useful, especially for growing or new products. For either a new or growing product, the adoption pattern of previous products of a similar type provides a clue as to both the likely pattern and rate of adoption, and the eventual saturation level.

The problem with using analogies is that two products are rarely perfectly comparable. For them to be reasonably comparable, it is desirable that both the newer product and its older analog be:

1. Targeted to a similar market.
2. Similar in perceived value, both in toto and in terms of the major benefits provided (e.g., convenience).
3. Similar in price.

Under these criteria, a microwave oven could be compared to a dishwasher (both are targeted at households, stress convenience/timesaving, and cost in the hundreds of dollars). By contrast, a mainframe computer (circa 1960) and a microcomputer (circa 1984) are not analogous, even though one is a direct descendant of the other, since the target market (a company versus individuals), value perceived (number crunching and billing versus convenience and word processing), and price (a million versus a few hundred dollars) are all dramatically different. Similarly, a home trash compactor and a dishwasher differed substantially on perceived value added and, therefore, a priori, one should have expected a much lower saturation level for trash compactors than for dishwashers.

Same Customer Sales

The more mature a product, the more sales will come from the past customers reordering the product. This reordering will come in two types. For a consumable product, the ordering of the product will be in proportion to the market need for their product (if an industrial product) or usage rate (if a consumer product). For a durable, ordering the product will be either (a) to replace a worn-out old product, (b) to upgrade to get new features, or (c) to add an additional model (e.g., a second color TV).

ESTIMATING MARKET AND SALES POTENTIAL: METHODS

The role of judgment in the derivation of potential elements is crucial and ubiquitous. It influences the type of data examined, the model used to derive the estimate, and often the estimate itself. While statistical knowledge is useful, logic or common sense is much more so. Therefore, the following methods are best viewed as aids to, rather than as substitutes for, judgment.

Pattern Extrapolation

For products where actual sales data are available, a common method of estimating potential is to use past data to project into the future. This can be done either by a simple examination of a graph of sales versus time, or by some mathematical model based on the first few sales periods (see the section on "Sales Forecasting Methods" for examples). A serious problem with this procedure is that both the eventual level and the rate at which it is achieved depend on elements of the product offering other than the physical product. For example, the potential for computers is clearly greater when the price is $3,000 rather than $3 million (Figure 6–4). Similarly, sales will tend to approach their ultimate level faster when more effort is put into selling the product (e.g., advertising or trade allowances). Also, the state of the economy will clearly have an impact on the sales of most goods and services. Thus, pattern extrapolation can be severely misleading if any of the elements of the marketing mix or the general environment are apt to change. Since production experience tends to decrease the cost and, therefore, the price of most goods, and high technology goods in particular, this suggests a more thorough analysis is needed even when actual data are available.

The most useful form of actual data is sales in regions geographically separated from the region under consideration. Here, projections of potential in a newly entered region can be made based on such variables as population in the target age group (for products such as foods) or number of businesses of a certain type (for products such as payroll services). Even when such regional information is available, however, the potential may differ widely for a variety of institutional and cultural reasons (e.g., the share of certain types of sterling silver flatware patterns varies widely among such areas as California, the South, and New England).

FIGURE 6–4
Relation of Potential to the Marketing Mix

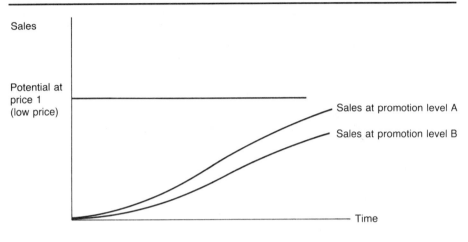

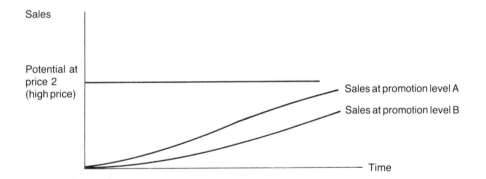

Analysis Based

In order to deduce the potential for a product, a basic approach is to first ascertain/estimate four things:

1. The type of people and/or organizations who might eventually buy the product category. This generally requires a careful analysis of the potential uses of the product and the relative value this product category has versus others in the various use situations.
2. The number of people and/or organizations of each type identified by 1. Generally, this is based on secondary data such as

population statistics or Department of Commerce data on businesses based on SIC codes.

3. The share of that type of people or business who will buy the product.
4. The rate at which buyers will consume the product (for a durable, this may be simply once).

Potential is then simply the product of 2, 3, and 4.

The foregoing four-step process is useful for getting an initial notion of a product's total potential. On the other hand, estimating the fraction who will buy in a broadly defined segment of the population and the rate at which they will consume is often very difficult.

Consider, for example, two products: a new copying system (an example of an industrial good) and a "diet" bourbon (a summer drink for the calorie conscious designed to compete with lighter alcoholic beverages such as vodka and wine coolers). Using the aggregate level analysis just described, we would estimate potential as follows:

New copying system potential: (Number of businesses) × (Percent who have copiers) × (Fraction who "need" our new feature) × (Share who will buy new system) × (Number bought per firm).

Diet bourbon potential: (Population over 21) × (Percent who drink bourbon) × (Percent who are diet conscious) × (Fraction who will buy diet bourbon) × (Purchase rate).

Notice that while both these examples are logical applications of the "successive ratio" approach suggested above, there is tremendous uncertainty in terms of defining "number of businesses" and "percent who are diet conscious," much less what share will buy the innovation. For that reason a segment-based approach as shown in Figure 6–5 is often useful for both predictive and diagnostic reasons.

Area Potential

Area potential is often derived by breaking down total sales by area. When sales data are available for a variety of regions along with some data on the characteristics of the regions, it is common to use an index of these characteristics to indicate the relative potential in the area. Many consumer goods companies use the *Sales and Marketing Management* Buying Power Index, which is: 0.2 (Population) + 0.3 (Retail sales) + 0.5 (Disposable income). This index is computed annually for the various

FIGURE 6–5

	Segment			
	(1) Number	(2) Vodka Consumption per Capita	(3) Percent Diet Conscious	(4) Consump- tion Rate	Segment Potential (1) × (2) × (3) × (4)
Diet bourbon:				
Single males 18–29				
Single females 18–29				
Married males 18–29				
Married females 18–29				
Single 30–55				
Married 30–55				
All 56 and older				
Total potential				

FIGURE 6–5 *(concluded)*

	Segment			
	(1)	(2)	(3)	(4)
	Number	Copier Use	Fraction Who Need Our Features	Number Needed per User	Segment Potential $(1) \times (2) \times (3) \times (4)$

New copying system:

Schools

Retail businesses

Banks

Offices

Warehouses

Manufacturing facilities

Other

Total potential

market areas of the United States. When population, retail sales, and disposable income are input as percent of the total United States, this index projects the percent of the product sold in the various regions. For established products, these weights may be estimated from the actual sales data by, for example, running a regression of sales versus the various factors (e.g., number of schools in region), and product-related data such as sales of analogous products (here Xerox copiers) might be used. In fact, sales of truly analogous products are often the best indicators of potential. An index approach for the hypothetical new copying system might then be employed as follows:

Bases: Percent population in region (P)
Percent schools in region (S)
Percent retail businesses in region (RB)
Percent banks in region (B)
Percent offices in region (O)
Percent warehouses in region (WH)
Percent manufacturing facilities in region (MF)
Percent other businesses in region (OB)
Percent Xerox sales in region (XS)
Percent other copier sales in region (CS)

$$Index = W_1P + W_2S + W_3RB + W_4B + W_5O + W_6WH \\ + W_7MF + W_8OB + W_9XS + W_{10}CS$$

A classical example of estimating area potential is provided by Hummel (1961) and described in Cox (1979). Hummel was concerned with estimating potential for a line of industrial truck casters manufactured by Bassick. Using trade association data (American Supply and Machinery Manufacturers Association) for class V products (power transmission equipment, industrial rubber goods, materials handling equipment), he found a close association between class V shipments and sales. Based on this, area potentials were estimated, and strong and weak market areas were identified.

Another example is related to sales of printing ink. Here sales were estimated for each user group based on the ratio of ink sales to total materials and supplies (Figure 6-6). For example, periodicals spent 3.5 percent of their material and supply budget on ink. Hence, the estimated San Francisco–Oakland SMSA printing ink sales would be ($7,600,000) × (.035) = $266,000.

One final example of market potential estimation deals with the

FIGURE 6–6
Market Potential for Printing Ink in the San Francisco–Oakland SMSA Area

| Industry | SIC Code | Materials Consumed, United States | | | San Francisco–Oakland SMSA | |
		All Materials and Supplies (millions)	Printing Inks (millions)	Proportion of Printing Inks to All Materials and Supplies	All Materials and Supplies (millions)	Market Potential ($)
Newspapers	2711	$1,438.2	$ 25.6	.018	$35.9	$ 646,200
Periodicals	2721	510.3	18.2	.035	7.6	266,000
Book publishing	2731	252.4	3.5	.014	3.8	53,200
Book printing	2732	224.4	11.5	.051	2.6	132,600
Commercial printing	275	2,112.3	139.3	.066	67.0	4,422,000
Manifold business forms	2761	348.9	4.4	.013	13.0	169,000
Total						$5,689,000

Note: Data on materials consumed, United States, drawn from *1967 Census of Manufacturers—Vol. I, Summary and Subject Statistics*; data on materials consumed in San Francisco–Oakland SMSA drawn from Vol. III, Part I of same *Census—Area Statistics*.

potential cargo volume for trucks between Atlanta and Los Angeles. One potential source of business would be beverages (SIC code 208). From the 1972 Census of Transportation the amount shipped from California to the Southeast region was 87,000 tons. Assuming we are estimating potential for 1975, this must be updated. The *Census of Manufacturers* indicates a 35.8 percent increase in dollar sales. Deflating by the cost-of-living increase of 23.2 percent, this suggests 1975 tons = (87,000) (1.358%) (1/1.232%) = 95,900. (Notice we have rounded off rather than to imply great precision.) Now it is necessary to convert general region-to-region shipment data into SMSA-to-SMSA shipment data. This could be done several ways, including using the census of manufacturing data on value-added and taking the ratio of Los Angeles SMSA to California and the Atlanta SMSA to the Southeast. The resulting market potential might then be: (95,900 tons) (Source ratio) (Destination ratio) = 9,050 tons.

In summary, market potential should be estimated systematically. Moreover, different approaches are needed for different situations (Table 6–1). Blind adherence to a system, however, will often result in a poor estimate. (The original projection showed a worldwide demand for main-frame computers of 15 to 20 and the demand for Xerox copiers under 2,000.) In short, both push numbers and think.

SALES FORECASTING METHODS

Conceptually, a sales forecast can be seen as an extension of the market potential estimate. For a new product, this can be derived as follows:

$$\frac{\text{Sales}}{\text{forecast}} = \frac{\text{Market}}{\text{potential}} \times \frac{\text{Percent of potential}}{\text{attained by}} \times \frac{\text{"Our" share}}{\text{of product}}$$
$$\text{product category} \quad \text{category}$$

For existing products this procedure is useful conceptually. For predictive purposes, however, it is more common to use actual sales data as the basis for the forecast. What the remainder of this section does, therefore, is describe some common methods for projecting sales and their pros and cons. There are three basic types of forecasting: qualitative, extrapolative (qualitative and quantitative), and model building. This section outlines some of the major alternatives of these three types.

TABLE 6–1
Suggested Approach to Estimating Potential for Different Situations

Situation	Key Data	Calculation Method
Relatively mature, stable, good	Past sales Judgment: is a critical change imminent?	Extrapolation
Growing product	Past sales Judgment: is a major competitive change imminent?	Extrapolation using a saturation level
New industrial good	Secondary: economic conditions Judgment: target segments (e.g., SIC codes)	Segment buildup
New consumer good: durable	Secondary: market segments (e.g., demographic) Survey plus judgment: rate of adoption	Segment buildup
New consumer good: frequently purchased	Secondary: market segments (demographic) Primary: Trial and report	New product forecasting model

Qualitative

Judgment
The least complicated forecasting method is the use of expert judgment (guessing might be a more appropriate description). Here we simply ask someone what the future will be and record the answer. If the expert chosen happens to know the Delphic Oracle or to be a mystic, the forecast may be excellent. Unfortunately, it is hard to know whether someone can predict the future a priori. The key to the value of expert judgment is the ability of the expert to recall from memory relevant data and assimilate the data in making a guess. While judgment is often unsystematic, it can be a very useful tool and can overcome some of the limitations of quantitative techniques. Probably the best use of judgment, however, is to adjust the results of quantitative procedures rather

than as the sole forecasting tool. Alternately, judgment-based decision trees of the type described in Chapter 2 can be used in developing forecasts.

Polling of Experts

The polling-of-experts method is really an extension of expert judgment under a safety-in-numbers assumption. Rather than trust a single expert, this approach collects forecasts from a number of experts. The forecasts are then combined in a particular manner, such as a simple or weighted average. (Since some experts are presumably more expert than others, their forecasts are weighted more heavily.) This method thus produces a forecast that is "neutral" and will (like most methods) avoid the unusual or radically different result. In fact, the most useful information from polling experts may be the range of the forecasts and the reasons given to support the forecasts rather than their average.

Panel Consensus

The panel consensus method of forecasting consists of putting a group of experts in a room and waiting for them to agree on a forecast. Aside from problems with dominant group members, this method will generally produce (assuming the panel members eventually agree) the conventional wisdom. Since experts sometimes have a habit of being wrong (e.g., remember the new math, stock market forecasts, and the impossibility of an international oil cartel?), the experts' opinions can be deceptively impressive.

A variety of "fancy" techniques are available for gaining panel consensus. One of the best known of these is the Delphi procedure, which is often used as a budget-setting method. The process begins by asking a number of individuals to allocate funds to a set of projects. An outside person then collects the allocations and calculates average allocations. Next, the outside person gives each participant back both the original allocation and the average allocations. At this point, each participant is asked to reconsider initial allocations. Typically (and hopefully), the participants then change their allocations to more nearly conform to the average. Therefore, if the process is repeated several times, consensus is achieved.

Survey Based

In estimating the demand for a product, a distinct approach is to conduct a survey of potential customers, who are after all "experts." While apparent, this approach is not without perils. For example, the usual issues of nonresponse bias and inaccurate responses arise. Moreover, two questions are especially troublesome. We will examine them here.

1. Who to Survey?   When conducting surveys for industrial products, it is not at all clear who to talk to within a company even if the company is known. For example, when the Federal Communication Commission (FCC) invited bids for cellular mobile phone licenses in various cities, it required a study of the market potential as part of the application. Most companies attempted to address this by phone surveys where the manager of telecommunications (or someone having a similar title) was contacted and asked how many phones the company would use. However, it is not clear that these managers knew how many were needed or had much authority over such acquisitions.

Regarding which companies to survey first requires specifying the potential segments and then ensuring there are enough of each type included to get a reasonable estimate. Unfortunately, if there are 10 target groups and 5 size variations per group, this leads to a large sample size.

Consider Table 6–2 which shows the number of firms by employee number in several SIC codes. How would you apportion the sample and still be able to represent each segment "accurately"? The answer requires a balance between a stratified sample based on assumed variability of demand and getting a reasonable number in each cell.

2. Dealing with the Results.   Considering again the example in Table 6–2, it would be preferable if the results "made sense," but sometimes they are inconsistent. For example, assume that the average firm sales for the five size categories in Table 6–1 were as follows: 192, 181, 490, 360, and 2,000.

Do you treat them as "truth," or do you smooth them so that bigger firms spend more? Moreover, what do you do if total demand comes out three times "expected"? Do you scale every estimate down by one third?

In summary, then, while surveys may produce a useful number, they are equally apt to produce numbers which, without "creative" manipulation, appear on the surface to be wrong.

Extrapolation: Qualitative

As a starting point for an alternative to expert judgment, a variety of extrapolation procedures exist. Two of these are essentially qualitative/judgmental in nature—last period + X percent and graphical eyeball.

TABLE 6-2
Potential Customers by Industry and Size

SIC	Industry	Percent of 1981 Demand Accounted For	Total Number of Firms	Number of Employees				
				50–99	100–249	250–499	500–999	1,000 or More
28	Chemical	20	7,012	754	610	293	193	123
29	Petroleum	20	444	57	73	53	42	22
33	Primary metals	10	1,889	266	352	181	74	108
12	Bituminous	2	4,050	295	272	166	80	11
20	Food	5	10,032	1,114	957	393	153	57
22	Textile	2	1,786	207	229	187	160	50
26	Paper and allied products	10	1,314	184	235	116	104	58
34	Fabricated metal	3	4,568	310	111	16	2	—
36	Electrical equipment	3	942	90	109	94	43	35
49	Electricity, gas	25	5,250	766	588	214	97	69
	Total		37,287	4,043	3,536	1,713	948	533

Expected Maximum Spending by Size Category

Employee Size	Maximum Spending
50 to 99	$ 100,000
100 to 249	200,000
250 to 499	500,000
500 to 999	750,000
1,000 or more	1,000,000

Last Period + X Percent

One of the most common approaches to forecasting is to estimate the percent change expected in the variable to be forecast. This is especially common in deriving annual sales forecasts for major product break-downs. For example, we may forecast dishwasher sales in dollars as last year's plus 6 percent.

Graphical Eyeball

Similar to the last period + *X* percent method, the graphical eyeball approach requires that past data be plotted. Then the next value is "eyeballed" to match the past pattern (Figure 6–7). As should be clear, this method does by graph what many quantitative techniques do by number crunching.

Extrapolation: Quantitative

A variety of quantitative extrapolation procedures are also available. Some of the most commonly used are given below.

Moving Average

Moving averages, an old forecasting standby, are widely used as a means of reducing the noise in data to uncover the underlying pattern. In doing so, it is important to recognize that past data has at least four major components:

FIGURE 6–7
Graphical Eyeball Forecasting

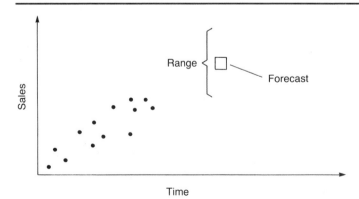

1. Base value.
2. Trend.
3. Cycle(s) (seasonality).
4. Random.

What moving averages essentially do is to smooth out random variation to make the patterns (trends and cycles) more apparent.

Complex moving-average models are available for estimating trends and cycles. For purposes of introduction, however, we will consider only the simple moving-average approach. A three-period moving average of sales at time t is given by

$$\hat{S}_t = \frac{S_{t-1} + S_t + S_{t+1}}{3}$$

Note this equation implies that (*a*) each data point used is weighted equally and (*b*) no trend or cycle is accounted for. To see how this method works, consider the three-month moving average for the eight periods of data in Table 6–3. As can be seen readily, the fluctuation in values is much less in moving averages than in the raw data, and a consistent trend of increase of about 10 units per period becomes quite apparent. Forecasts would now be based on the pattern of the moving averages rather than the raw data.

Moving-average methods can be extended to track trends and seasonal patterns as well. For example, in order to smooth a trend, simply calculate the period-to-period changes and average them as in Table 6–3. However, regression analysis (to be discussed later) has gener-

TABLE 6–3

Period	Sales	Three-Period Moving Average	Trend	Three-Period Trend Average
1	100	—	—	—
2	110	105	+ 10	—
3	105	115	− 5	+ 10
4	130	125	+ 25	− 10
5	140	130	+ 10	+ 5
6	120	140	− 20	+ 10
7	160	152	+ 40	+ 11.33
8	175	—	+ 15	—

ally replaced moving averages as a forecasting tool for all but the simplest situations.

Exponential Smoothing

A second major approach to extrapolation is exponential smoothing. As in the case of moving averages, this approach literally smooths out the random variation in period-to-period values. Also like moving averages, trends and cycles must be estimated (smoothed) separately. Data involving cycles and trends are handled by means of regression analysis rather than exponential smoothing.

Time Series Regression

A third way to extrapolate data is by using regression analysis with time (period) as the independent variable. Time series regression produces estimates of the base level (intercept) and trend (slope). Seasonal patterns can be handled outside the regression (i.e., by removing the estimated seasonal component from the values of the dependent variable before performing the regression), or by various "tricks" within the regression (e.g., using dummy variables; see Wildt, 1977). Ignoring seasonality, the model is simply

$$\text{Sales} = a + b(\text{Time})$$

Addressing the same eight-period example in this manner produces the result of Table 6–4. The forecast for period 10 based on this model would thus be

TABLE 6–4
Time Series Regression Example

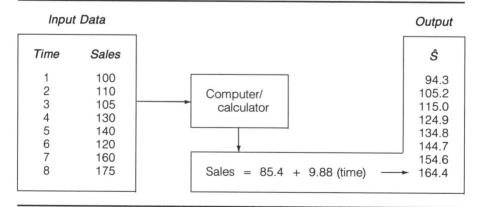

$$\hat{S}_{10} = 85.4 + 9.88(10) = 184.2$$

In addition to the basic forecast, regression produces several bonuses, including:

Measure of Goodness of Fit. R^2, which is percent of variance in sales which was explained.

Standard Error of Estimate. $S_{Y.X}$, which serves to quantify the range of likely outcomes. Typically, a prediction is given by $\hat{S} \pm KS_{Y.X}$. (For most situations, $K = 2$ will prove adequate.)

Actually, all three methods, moving average, exponential smoothing, and time series regressions, are very similar. They differ in which past results they use to develop their estimates. Moving averages weight some of the most recent data points equally. Exponential smoothing weights all the data points unequally with the most recent having the most weight, the next most recent the next highest weight, and so forth. Finally, regression typically weights all the points equally, although unequal weights can be used. Choice among the three is therefore a matter of taste, availability, and experience. Given our familiarity with regression, we use regression when the choice arises. More advanced forms of times series analysis such as Box-Jenkins methods are beyond the scope of this book. (See Appendix A for a more complete discussion of time series regression.)

Model-Based Forecasting

Model-based forecasting approaches are distinguished from extrapolative procedures in that in addition to using past data for the item being forecast, they assume that future results will occur based on either a particular pattern or set of influences. The most common model forms are epidemic and regression models.

Epidemic Models

An approach to forecasting sales of a new product is to assume that initial sales of the product will follow the same shape curve (Figure 6–8) as an epidemic (which, given some new products, may be an apt analogy). This curve implies that there will be a slow start during which the innovators become "infected," followed by a growth period in which sales of the product (or the disease) spread rapidly through the population. Sales then slow down as the number of eventual buyers (people

FIGURE 6–8
Trial over Time for a New Product

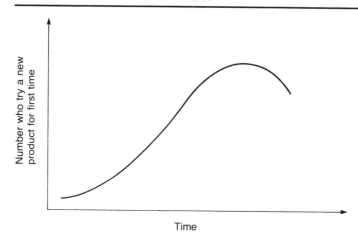

susceptible to the disease) is approached. Such a model has been presented by Bass (1969) and used in companies such as Eastman Kodak to
forecast sales of new consumer durables in terms of when they would
peak and how big the peak would be. While such models may be imper-
fect predictors, the basic notion of a pattern of sales growth over time
and the existence of a saturation level are useful in considering any type
of forecast. (See Appendix B for a more detailed discussion of epidemic
models.)

Regression Models
Regression models are the most widely used form of models in marketing
research. These models are developed in three stages. First, the variables
that are assumed to affect the dependent variable are specified as:

Sales $= f$(Our price, competitors' prices, our advertising,
competitors' advertising, disposable income)

Next, a model that indicates the form of the relation between the
independent variables and sales is specified. These models are generally
linear, such as:

Sales in cartons (S) = Constant
$+ B_1$ (Our price)
$+ B_2$ (Our advertising)
$+ B_3$ (Disposable income)

The model is then estimated by means of regression analysis:

$$S = 1.2 - .2 \, (\text{Price in dollars}) + 1.3 \, (\text{Advertising in dollars})$$
$$+ .1 \, (\text{Disposable income in \$ billions})$$

Regression models serve two basic uses which we discuss at this point.

1. Sales Forecasting. Notice that to use regression models to forecast, one must first forecast the values of the independent variables. If this is difficult, then regression becomes less useful as a straight forecasting device. Put differently, in building a multiple-regression model for purposes of forecasting, make sure that the independent variables are easily forecast. Also, every forecast should have a range. Typically a range of about two standard errors of estimate is used.

2. Answering "What If" Questions. In our example,

$$B_1 = \text{Marginal effect of changing our price}$$
$$B_2 = \text{Marginal effect of changing our advertising share}$$

If you make the rather large assumption that the relation between price and sales is causal rather than just correlational, you can answer a question such as "What if I increase advertising by \$10?" In this case, a \$10 increase in advertising would lead to a $(1.3)(10) = 13$ carton change in sales.

Selection of Variables

The criteria for which variables to include in a regression model are numerous, including the following:

1. Parsimony (bosses like simple models).
2. Data availability (available data typically dictates variable selection).
3. Plausibility (Do the independent variables logically affect the dependent variable and are the forecasts reasonable?).
4. Goodness of fit (Does the independent variable help predict the dependent variable? Bosses hate low R^2s).
5. "Good" coefficients (Are the signs and magnitudes of the coefficients reasonable?).

Given these multiple criteria, it is not surprising that building regression models is a trial-and-error process. In terms of the type of variables to include, it is generally useful to consider what variables in each of the following categories might be most appropriate.

1. Customer status and traits (e.g., age distribution of the population).
2. Competitive behavior (e.g., new product introductions).
3. "Our" marketing programs (e.g., advertising).
4. General environment (e.g., gross national product).

Simultaneous Equation Models

In order to improve the accuracy of a forecast for a particularly important variable (e.g., oil prices), it is often necessary to take into account the interactions between this variable and other variables. For example, the price of oil influences the price of food, and the price of food influences the price of oil. In order to model such interdependency, systems of equations are specified. The parameters of these models are then estimated by simultaneous equation regression. Using these models requires considerable development cost and technical know-how, and therefore they are used only in limited circumstances.

CHOICE OF FORECASTING METHODS

The time horizon has a major effect on the appropriate forecasting method(s) to choose and the accuracy one can expect. Put bluntly, anything will do to predict next week (with exceptions—e.g., umbrellas), and nothing can predict 30 years ahead. The relation between the time horizon of the forecast and the method to be used can be summarized as follows:

Term of Forecast	"Best" Method
1. Short (less than 6 months)	Simple extrapolation
2. Medium (1–5 years)	Quantitative (regression)
3. Long (5–30 years)	Model building and mystic
4. Super long (30 years and up)	Flip a coin, no one knows

Expressed differently, it is difficult to say which techniques are good and which are bad since it often depends on the circumstances involved. Still, comparisons are useful, and the summary provided by Chambers, Mullick, and Smith (1974) is widely viewed as an excellent summary. A recent comparison of methods appears in Georgoff and Murdick (1986).

Using quantitative procedures may at times seem tedious. Still, there are several reasons why quantitative methods are beneficial: (1) they simplify routine, repetitive situations, and (2) force explicit statements of assumptions. When using quantitative procedures, it is best to use the following steps.

1. *Graph the data if possible.* "A picture may be worth a thousand analyses." As an example of how important a picture can be, consider again the eight-period example of Table 6–3. Graphed, the data look like Figure 6–9. An interesting pattern thus emerges: two up periods, followed by a down period. While this pattern is only three cycles old, it does suggest that a forecast in the 130 to 140 area for period 9 would be supportable. This pattern can be overlooked by simple number crunching.

FIGURE 6–9
Plot of Sales Data Example

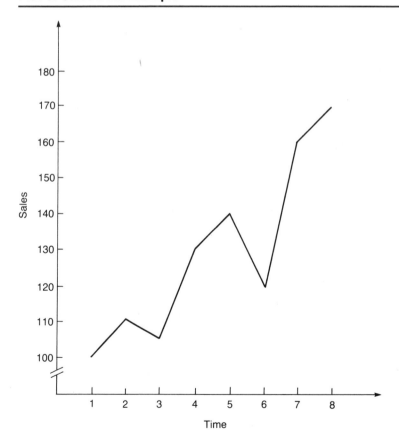

2. *Do sensitivity analysis.*   Only when a result seems to be stable over method and data points (drop one or two points and rerun the analysis), can the forecast be advanced with much conviction.
3. *Examine big "residuals."*   By examining the characteristics of those periods (data points) when the forecast was bad, omitted variables can often be uncovered.
4. *Avoid silly precision.*   This means rounding off the forecast and giving an honest plus or minus range.
5. *Be tolerant of errors.*   Expect the methods to improve one's odds of making a good forecast, not to guarantee them.
6. *Remember you will generally miss all the turning points.*   Quantitative (as well as qualitative) forecasting methods work well as long as the patterns that occurred in the past extend into the future. Whenever a major change occurs, however, most forecasts will be way off. Stated another way, most forecasting methods are generally useless for predicting major changes in the way the world operates (oil embargoes, changes in social values, and so on), and consequently the effects of these changes are not included in most forecasts.

EXAMPLE: THE YEAR 2000

In 1970, a problem was posed which was, in essence, "What will the effect of different U.S. populations be on U.S. industries in the year 2000?" Given this rather nebulous topic, the decision was made to build a model of unit sales for 19 industries based on, among other things, population. A variety of approaches were considered and rejected:

1. Input-output analysis. (The researcher didn't know enough about it.)
2. Simultaneous equation regression models. (Insufficient time and budget.)
3. Index numbers. (Not enough experience with, too subjective.)

That left two good standbys: (1) single equation regression, and (2) polling of experts.

The major thrust was to use a single equation model for each of the 19 industries. Also, 35 experts were asked to indicate what they felt would happen to sales in the 19 industries under different population assumptions (Howard & Lehmann, 1971). These judgments were used mainly to backstop the quantitative methods and served to help eliminate predictions that would not be believable. (Having believable predictions tends to increase the speed with which a consultant gets paid.)

A wide variety of potential regression models is available. There being no particular reason for choosing a particular one, a number were investigated (see Figure 6–10).

The results were then examined and the best model chosen. Almost without exception, the lagged models and first difference models produced "funny" results when extrapolated 30 years into the future based on the data used (1948–69 and 1959–69). In fact, the "best" results seemed to come from using the 1959–69 data on model 2:

$$\text{Sales} = B_0 + B_1(\text{POP}_t) + B_2 \frac{\text{DI}_t}{\text{CPI}_t}$$

The resulting equations were then used for forecasting unit sales in the year 2000 under two population estimates and two disposable income estimates. The results clearly illustrate the frustration of forecasting 30 years into the future based on 11 years' worth of data. First, the supposedly "low" population estimate at the time was 266,281,000, a number that currently appears, if anything, high. Second, it is hard to believe that some of the projections will come true. The best example of this is automobiles, where the forecasts for the year 2000 based on the lower population and disposable income estimates were as follows:

Domestic	1.2 million
Imported	19 million

This result is hard to believe on two counts. First, it is difficult to project sales of 20 million cars in the year 2000 (at least cars as we know them today). Second, it seems unlikely that imported cars will be allowed (either by GM or other car manufacturers, or the U.S. government) to so totally dominate the market. (It may be, however, that small cars will have such a dominant share.) This prediction is the result of the linear extrapolation of the past trend over a long period of time. While linear extrapolations work well in the short run, they tend to be off in the long run. The point, therefore, is that these estimates cannot be maintained with much certainty (Would you believe a confidence interval of zero to infinity?). That doesn't mean that long-range forecasts aren't important; airports, utilities, and so forth, all need to plan many years into the future. What it does mean is that anyone doing long-range forecasting deserves credit for courage and some sympathy.

FIGURE 6–10
Alternative Models of Sales as a Function of Population

1. $S_t = B_0 + B_1(POP_t)$

2. $S_t = B_0 + B_1(POP_t) + B_2\left(\dfrac{DI_t}{CPI_t}\right)$

3. $S_t = B_0 + B_1(POP_t) + B_2\left(\dfrac{DI_t}{CPI_t} \div POP_t\right)$

4. $S_t = B_0 + B_1(t) + B_2(POP_t) + B_3(DI_t/CPI_t)$

5. $S_t = B_0 + B_1(t) + B_2(POP_t) + B_3\left(\dfrac{DI_t}{CPI_t} \div POP_t\right)$

6. $S_t = B_0 + B_1(t) + B_2(POP_t)$

One-year lags

7. $S_t = B_0 + B_1(POP_{t-1})$

8. $S_t = B_0 + B_1(POP_{t-1}) + B_2(DI_{t-1}/CPI_{t-1})$

9. $S_t = B_0 + B_1(POP_{t-1}) + B_2\left(\dfrac{DI_t}{CPI_t} \div POP_{t-1}\right)$

10. $S_t = B_0 + B_1(t-1) + B_2(POP_{t-1}) + B_3(DI_{t-1}/CPI_{t-1})$

11. $S_t = B_0 + B_1(t-1) + B_2(POP_{t-1}) + B_3\left(\dfrac{DI_{t-1}}{CPI_{t-1}} \div POP_{t-1}\right)$

12. $S_t = B_0 + B_1(t-1) + B_2(POP_{t-1})$

Five-year lags

13. $S_t = B_0 + B_1(POP_{t-5})$

14. $S_t = B_0 + B_1(POP_{t-5}) + B_2(DI_{t-5}/CPI_{t-5})$

15. $S_t = B_0 + B_1(POP_{t-5}) + B_2\left(\dfrac{DI_{t-5}}{CPI_{t-5}} \div POP_{t-5}\right)$

16. $S_t = B_0 + B_1(t-5) + B_2(POP_{t-5}) + B_3(DI_{t-5}/CPI_{t-5})$

17. $S_t = B_0 + B_1(t-5) + B_2(POP_{t-5}) + B_3\left(\dfrac{DI_{t-5}}{CPI_{t-5}} \div POP_{t-5}\right)$

18. $S_t = B_0 + B_1(t-5) + B_2(POP_{t-5})$

First differences

19. $(S_t - S_{t-1}) = B_0 + B_1(POP_t - POP_{t-1})$

20. $(S_t - S_{t-1}) = B_0 + B_1(POP_t - POP_{t-1}) + B_2\left(\dfrac{DI_t}{CPI_t} - \dfrac{DI_{t-1}}{CPI_{t-1}}\right)$

21. $(S_t - S_{t-1}) = B_0 + B_1(POP_t - POP_{t-1})$
$$+ B_2\left(\dfrac{DI_t}{CPI_t} \div POP_t - \dfrac{DI_{t-1}}{CPI_{t-1}} \div POP_{t-1}\right)$$

FIGURE 6–10 (concluded)

Logs*

22. $\log S_t = B_0 + B_1 \log(\text{POP}_t) + B_2 \log(\text{DI}_t/\text{CPI}_t)$

23. $\log S_t = B_0 + B_1 \log(\text{POP}_t) + B_2 \log\left(\dfrac{\text{DI}_t}{\text{CPI}_t} \div \text{POP}_t\right)$

Logs, one-year lags

24. $\log S_t = B_0 + B_1 \log(\text{POP}_{t-1}) + B_2 \log(\text{DI}_{t-1}/\text{CPI}_{t-1})$

25. $\log S_t = B_0 + B_1 \log(\text{POP}_{t-1}) + B_2 \log\left(\dfrac{\text{DI}_{t-1}}{\text{CPI}_{t-1}} \div \text{POP}_{t-1}\right)$

Logs, five-year lags

26. $\log S_t = B_0 + B_1 \log(\text{POP}_{t-5}) + B_2 \log(\text{DI}_{t-5}/\text{CPI}_{t-5})$

27. $\log S_t = B_0 + B_1 \log(\text{POP}_{t-5}) + B_1 \log\left(\dfrac{\text{DI}_{t-5}}{\text{CPI}_{t-5}} \div \text{POP}_{t-5}\right)$

S = Sales
POP = Population
DI = Disposable income
CPI = Total consumer price index
t = Time (year)

*This implies $S_t = B_0(\text{POP}_t)^{B_1}(\text{DI}_t/\text{CPI}_t)^{B_2}$

GAINING AGREEMENT

The previous sections have focused mainly on top-down forecasting, that is, a forecast made by a staffperson. Often forecasts are bottom-up in nature where various individuals (salespeople, division managers) make forecasts for their particular area and these forecasts are then aggregated. Unfortunately, top-down and bottom-up forecasts rarely agree. The process of reaching agreement is both useful and frustrating.

In understanding bottom-up forecasts, it is useful to recognize that both personal incomes and budgets depend on the forecast. Personal incomes, especially of salespeople, are tied to quotas which in turn are derived from forecasts. Therefore, a salesperson will tend to be conservative in his or her forecast in order to make the sales goal or quota easier to attain. By contrast, certain managers may overstate sales potential in order to gain a bigger budget. Thus, the bottom-up process, though based on the knowledge of those closest to the customer, may well produce a biased estimate. Therefore, total reliance on either bottom-up or top-down methods is generally a mistake.

Typically, then, forecasting may involve an iterative procedure where top-down and bottom-up forecasts are reconciled into a "negotiated" settlement.

Combining Forecasts

So far this chapter has described a number of forecasting methods and their strengths and weaknesses. In practice, when making an important forecast it is both common and prudent to make several forecasts and then combine them. Put differently, the issue is not to decide which is the best forecast, but to create a forecast which combines the available forecasts. For example, in producing an industry forecast one should generally do the following:

1. Plot the data and extrapolate. Normally, for mature industries a linear extrapolation will suffice whereas for new industries a nonlinear procedure (such as the Base model) which explicitly recognizes the eventual saturation level is often useful.
2. Build a regression model which includes independent variables that are, as much as possible,
   a. Good predictors.
   b. Uncorrelated with each other.
   c. Easy to forecast themselves.

This model will generally include general economic variables (e.g., GNP, population) as well as industry variables (e.g., average price if it has been changing).
3. Collect forecasts available from others (e.g., security analysts).
4. Provide a subjective forecast based on consideration of likely future changes and their impact on sales.
5. Create a bottom-up forecast by summing up, for example, district managers' forecasts.

The range of these forecasts provides a useful indication of the uncertainty faced. Moreover, deciding how to combine these forecasts forces one to make explicit assumptions.

Recently a number of researchers have addressed the issue of the optimal way to combine forecasts. The best way is to weight forecasts based on their relative accuracy. Unless there is great variation in accuracy, therefore, an equal weighting works quite well.

SUMMARY

Since potential is a future-oriented concept, it is vital (but not always recognized as such) to consider the impact of future changes on the marketplace. These include all of the assumptions about the environment, including the economy, regulation, competitors, and so on. While many times such considerations may not materially affect the potential estimate or forecast, failure to take them into account will almost ensure that some major turning points in a market will be missed. Since one of the major objectives of planning is to reduce surprises, at least a casual future scanning is strongly recommended.

In presenting forecasts, it is desirable to indicate the level of uncertainty involved. This requires recognition of uncertainty concerning market conditions (e.g., state of the economy) as well as uncertainty given a set of conditions. A simple form of such a presentation is shown in Figure 6–11.

One advantage of Figure 6–11 is that it highlights the key determinants of the forecast (often uncovered in a regression analysis) in the scenarios in a nontechnical way. Another advantage is by presenting both a best guess and low and high estimates (again, these can be based on a regression analysis by adding and subtracting standard errors from the best guess prediction), the level of uncertainty is made clearer.

FIGURE 6–11
A Format for Presenting Forecasts

Scenario	Low Estimate	Best Guess	High Estimate
Maximum potential (fast GNP growth, and so on)			
Best guess (moderate growth in GNP, and so on)			
Minimum potential (no growth in GNP, and so on)			

Finally, it is crucial to recognize that forecasting is a trying undertaking. Besides a sense of security and humor, the following are useful tools:

1. Understanding of:
   a. The problem.
   b. The situation.
2. Common sense.
3. Willingness to live with uncertainty. (False precision costs money since it doesn't encourage proper contingency planning.)
4. A number cruncher (the ability to use quantitative methods).
5. A coin. At some point in the forecasting process, a guess will need to be made. By using a coin, you can blame the result on someone or something else (e.g., a consultant, whom you can at least have the satisfaction of firing before your pink slip arrives).

APPENDIX A TIME SERIES REGRESSION WITH SEASONAL FACTORS

Consider the following data on quarterly fuel oil shipments to the United Kingdom in 1964–66 (Table A–1). In plotting this data, we see that there is, as expected, a very strong seasonal trend (Figure A–1). Clearly, ignoring the seasonal component would be a major error. (It would also produce significant autocorrelation.) Running four separate regressions is impractical because there would only be three observations per regression. It would be possible to de-seasonalize the data before performing the regression, using an adjustment factor for each quarter such as

TABLE A–1
Fuel Oil Shipments to the United Kingdom

Quarter	Year	Sales
1	1964	210
2		120
3		140
4		260
1	1965	220
2		125
3		145
4		270
1	1966	225
2		128
3		149
4		275

FIGURE A–1

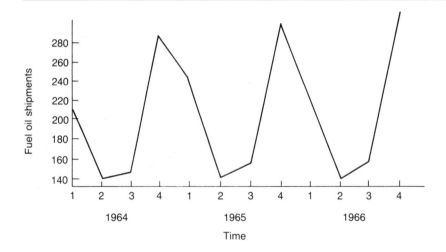

$$\frac{\text{Average sales for the particular quarter}}{\text{Average sales for all quarters}}$$

Possibly the most appealing approach, however, is to employ dummy variables. This would consist of first creating ("dummying up") a variable for each of the four quarters (Table A–2). The following equation would then be estimated by regression:

$$\text{Shipments} = B_0 + B_1\,(\text{Time}) + B_2\,(\text{Winter})$$
$$+ B_3\,(\text{Spring}) + B_4\,(\text{Summer})$$

Note that one of the possible dummy variables must be left out so the computer program will run. If all the independent variables are included, the independent variables are perfectly multicollinear. In this case it is impossible to invert a key matrix and the program will bomb. (Alternatively, we could drop the constant B_0 and retain all four dummy variables, if that were an option of the computer program being used.) In general, if a categorical variable has c categories, $c-1$ dummy variables must be employed. Here, fall was excluded. This does not affect the final interpretation of the results, which are independent of the variable deleted. The results were:

$$B_0 = 256.5$$
$$B_1 = 1.468$$
$$B_2 = -45.6$$
$$B_3 = -141.1$$
$$B_4 = -122.2$$

Predictions for each of the quarters are thus:

$$\text{Winter:} \qquad \text{Shipments} = B_0 + B_1\,(\text{Time}) + B_2\,(1)$$
$$+ B_3\,(0) + B_4\,(0)$$
$$= (B_0 + B_2) + B_1\,(\text{Time})$$
$$= 210 + 1.468\,(\text{Time})$$

TABLE A–2

| Shipments | Time | Dummy Variables | | | |
		Winter	Spring	Summer	Fall
210	1	1	0	0	0
120	2	0	1	0	0
140	3	0	0	1	0
260	4	0	0	0	1
220	5	1	0	0	0
125	6	0	1	0	0
145	7	0	0	1	0
270	8	0	0	0	1
225	9	1	0	0	0
128	10	0	1	0	0
149	11	0	0	1	0
275	12	0	0	0	1

Spring: Shipments $= (B_0 + B_3) + B_1$ (Time)
$= 115.5 + 1.468$ (Time)

Summer: Shipments $= (B_0 + B_4) + B_1$ (Time)
$= 134.4 + 1.468$ (Time)

Fall: Shipments $= B_0 + B_1$ (Time)
$= 256.6 + 1.468$ (Time)

The results are shown graphically as Figure A–2. The coefficients of the dummy variables are interpreted as the difference in the average value of the dependent variable between the category of the dummy variable and the category of the variable which has no dummy variable. Thus,

$$B_2 = \frac{210 + 220 + 225}{3} - \frac{260 + 270 + 275}{3}$$

$$= -50 = -45.6 - 3(1.468)$$

Here the coefficients of the dummy variables indicate the difference in average sales between each quarter and the fall quarter. For example, average shipments in the spring are 45.6 less than shipments in the fall.

If this model were used to predict shipments in the second quarter of 1968, the "best guess" prediction would then be

Predicted shipments $= 155.5 + 1.468(18) = 142$

FIGURE A–2

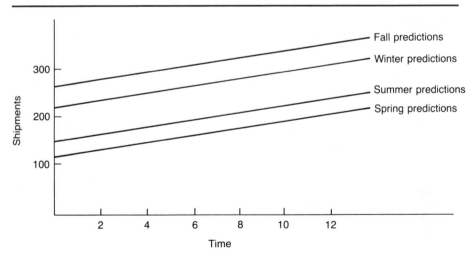

DEALING WITH OUTLIERS

Anyone dealing with forecasting soon discovers that in most data sets a few observations often appear that are very far from the forecast value. The question that immediately rises is what to do with them. Actually, two very different answers appear: Spend some time attempting to explain the outliers or reduce their impact on the forecast by "neutralizing" them.

Studying Them

This approach is often the most useful since frequently the outliers contain substantial information. For example, if a sales versus potential regression were run with data on 79 territories, sales in some of the territories could be abnormally low or high. By examining the characteristics of the "outliers," one often discovers an explanation that leads to altering the model by adding one or more additional variables to it. In fact, examination of outliers is often the most expedient way to consider model modification.

Neutralizing Them

Assuming either (*a*) no explanation can be found for outliers, suggesting they are simply unusual, random happenings; (*b*) an explanation can be found that is hopefully or genuinely a one-time occurrence (e.g., the problem at Three Mile Island); or (*c*) the forecast is not critical (e.g., a very minor product), then it may be more beneficial simply to remove them. One way of doing this is to just ignore their impact which will work if they are randomly distributed (Figure A–3A). Unfortunately, a small number of "grouped" outliers, as in Figure A–3B, can severely distort the forecast line and hence the forecasts. Therefore, it is often useful to reduce their impact on the forecast.

Reducing the impact on the forecast is typically done by replacing the actual value with a value that is closer to the value one would expect based on the other observations. This data manipulation can range from the extreme of substituting the forecast for the actual to the less severe "filtering" approaches that replace the actual data with, for example, the 95 percent confidence interval value for the observation. A more extreme approach is to simply disregard the observation. In addition to seeming "unfair," all these approaches run the risk of producing results (e.g., R^2s) that are falsely impressive and hence lead the user of the forecast to underestimate the uncertainty that exists.

When the identity of the outlier is known and the cause deduced, it is possible to subjectively adjust the actual value by the impact of the cause. For example, one might assume that a strike which lasted one of four weeks in a

FIGURE A-3

A. Random outliers

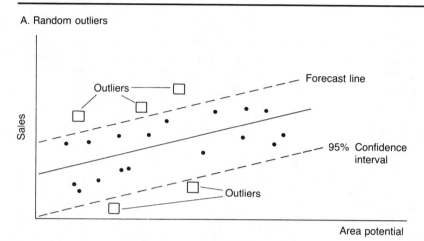

B. Grouped outliers

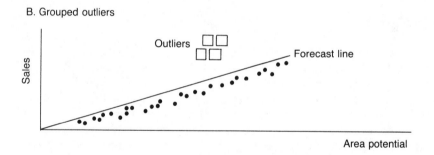

given period reduced sales by 25 percent; consequently, we would multiply actual sales by 1.33 to get actual sales as they would have been without the strike. (Notice that this assumes no carryover effects of sales across periods, which for all but the most perishable commodities—for example, fresh melon, newspaper—is a bad assumption.) While this approach is subjective, if the goal is to produce forecasts based on the underlying trend, then such manipulation may be the most appropriate way to produce believable forecasts.

APPENDIX B   EPIDEMIC MODELS OF INITIAL SALES

A general form of the epidemic model is given by:

$$P(\text{Buy/Not previously bought}) \;+\; a + bF + c(1-F) + dF(1-F)$$

where $F = Y(t) = $ Cumulative sales. Most popular diffusion models are a special case of this. For example, the Bass model assumed c and $d = 0$.

The model used by Bass has the following form:

$$p(t) \;=\; p + \frac{q}{M}\, Y(t)$$

where

> $p(t)$ = Probability of purchase given no previous purchase was made
> $Y(t)$ = Total number who have tried
> M = Total number of potential buyers (saturation level)
> q = Parameter reflecting the rate of diffusion of the product
> p = Initial probability of purchase

Thus,

$$S(t) \;=\; [M - Y(t)]\,p(t)$$
$$= pM + [q-p]\,Y(t) - \frac{q}{M}\,[Y(t)]^2$$

The model can be estimated by running a regression of current versus past sales:

$$S(t) \;=\; c_0 + c_1\,Y(t) + c_2\,[Y(t)]^2$$

This model has fit past adoption patterns quite well. For example, it correctly forecast a downturn in sales of color TVs in the late 1960s, something which the "expert" forecasts at the major manufacturers failed to do because of their use of essentially linear extrapolation. Unfortunately, the model is sensitive to data points and therefore unreliable when only four or five data points (e.g., years of sales) are available. The simple models also ignore marketing variables. For example, the saturation level M probably depends on price, which often declines over time, and the purchase rate $p(t)$ depends on distribution, advertising, and so on.

Also, it has been pointed out that estimating this model separately for major segments noticeably improves predictive power (Wind, Robertson, & Fraser, 1982).

While the Bass model of sales over time has some appealing behavioral justification, a variety of alternative models is available. These include:

1. Exponential.   By assuming $S(t) = a + be^{-t}$, a curve projecting sales is derived.

2. Weibull. The Weibull distribution is widely used to predict product failure, and it is frequently used in marketing as an alternative to the Bass model. Usually, the Weibull and Bass models produce fairly similar results. The model is

$$S(e) = \frac{bt^{b-1}}{a} \exp \frac{(-t^b)}{a}$$

or

$$Y(t) = 1 - \exp \frac{(-t^b)}{a}$$

3. Technological Substitution. One interesting approach to projecting the impact of a new (and presumably better) technology is to examine the rate at which it replaces the old technology. The simplest of such models assume that eventually (at least for some segments) substitution will be complete. One model of the substitution process was developed by Fisher and Pry (1971) and discussed extensively by Cooper and Schendel (1976). The model is based on the assumption that the fraction (f) who will adopt the new technology is given by

$$\frac{df}{df} = 2\alpha \frac{f}{(1-f)}$$

This leads to

$$f = \frac{1}{2}[1 + \tanh \alpha (t - t_0)]$$

The model has been shown to fit a number of situations, including open hearth versus Bessemer steel production, water- versus oil-based paints, and plastic versus metal in automobiles. Consequently, if one has a few years of data for a new product, one can separately forecast the fraction (f) who will use the new product and the size of the total market (new plus old), which may be essentially constant, and then estimate potential of the new product by multiplying f times total market. While this model obviously does not consider (*a*) changes in the marketing mixes of makers of the two product types, (*b*) increases in primary demand due to the properties of the new product, or (*c*) measurement issues such as appropriate units (e.g., pounds, dollars, number of applications), it still provides a useful benchmark for potential estimates. Fisher and Pry (1971) also observed the following:

1. Sales of the old product may initially continue to expand and generally did.
2. The time until the old product was replaced by the new as the sales leader was 5–14 years.
3. The initial model of the new product was crude and expensive, which led to an underestimation of its potential.
4. The new product "overpowers" the old market segment by segment rather than across the board.

REFERENCES

Bass, Frank M. "A New Product Growth for Model Consumer Durables." *Management Science* 15 (January 1969), pp. 215–27.

Chambers, John C.; Satinder K. Mullick; and Donald D. Smith. "How to Choose the Right Forecasting Technique." *Harvard Business Review* 49 (July–August 1971), pp. 45–74.

Chambers, John C.; Satinder K. Mullick; and Donald D. Smith. *An Executives Guide to Forecasting.* New York: John Wiley & Sons, 1974.

Cooper, Arnold C., and Dan Schendel. "Strategic Responses to Technological Threats." *Business Horizons,* February 1976, pp. 61–69.

Cox, William E., Jr., and George N. Havens. "Determination of Sales Potentials and Performance for an Industrial Goods Manufacturer." *Journal of Marketing Research* 14 (November 1977), pp. 574–78.

Cox, William E., Jr. *Industrial Marketing Research.* New York: Ronald Press, 1979.

Draper, N., and H. Smith. *Applied Regression Analysis.* New York: John Wiley & Sons, 1966.

Fisher, J. C., and R. H. Pry. "A Simple Substitution Model of Technological Threats." *Technological Forecasting and Social Change* 3 (1971), pp. 75–88.

Georgoff, David M., and Robert G. Murdick. "Manager's Guide to Forecasting." *Harvard Business Review* 64 (January–February 1986), pp. 110–20.

Howard, John A., and Donald R. Lehmann. "The Effect of Different Populations on Selected Industries in the Year 2000." Commission on Population Growth and the American Future, Research Reports, Vol. II, *Economic Aspects of Populations Change,* ed. Elliot R. Morse and Ritchie H. Reed. Washington, D.C.: United States Commission on Population Growth and the American Future, pp. 145–58.

Hummel, Francis E. *Market and Sales Potentials.* New York: Ronald Press, 1961.

Lehmann, Donald R. *Market Research and Analysis.* Homewood, Ill.: Richard D. Irwin, 1985.

McLaughlin, Robert L. "The Breakthrough in Sales Forecasting." *Journal of Marketing* 27 (April 1963), pp. 46–54.

McLaughlin, Robert L., and J. J. Boyle. *Short-Term Forecasting.* Chicago: American Marketing Association, 1968.

Pessemier, Edgar A. *Product Management.* New York: John Wiley & Sons, 1977.

Stern, Mark E. *Market Planning.* New York: McGraw-Hill, 1966.

Tull, Donald S., and Del I. Hawkins. *Marketing Research.* New York: Macmillan, 1976.

Urban, Glen L., and John R. Hauser. *Design and Marketing of New Products.* Englewood Cliffs, N.J.: Prentice-Hall, 1980.

Wheelwright, Steven C., and Spyros Makridakis. *Forecasting Methods for Management*. New York: John Wiley & Sons, 1985.

Wildt, Albert R. "Estimating Models of Seasonal Market Response Using Dummy Variables." *Journal of Marketing Research* 14 (February 1977), pp. 34–41.

Wind, Yoram; Thomas S. Robertson; and Cynthia Fraser. "Industrial Product Diffusion by Market Segment." *Industrial Marketing Management* 11 (1982), pp. 1–8.

CHAPTER 7

INTEGRATING THE INFORMATION

OVERVIEW

The preceding chapters of this book have been devoted to a discussion of the types of data and analyses required to develop marketing objectives, strategies, and tactics. As can easily be seen, the kind of information required is different for the various analyses and ranges from demographic trend data to competitor information. What is ultimately needed is a way to tie together all the different analyses in a way that managers can develop marketing strategies. In other words, how can the competitor, customer, and industry analyses, together with the forecasts and market potential estimates, be used simultaneously to help the marketing manager make decisions?

In this final chapter, we briefly discuss methods for assimilating this diverse information. We first discuss the creation of an information system structure for handling the planning process. Two major approaches to using the information are subsequently described: (1) scenario analysis, a qualitative approach for developing strategic plans based on uncertainty; and (2) a quantitative approach using a decision support system. We conclude the book with a look at the future of marketing planning in terms of artificial intelligence-based expert systems.

DEVELOPING A PLANNING SYSTEM

To be best able to reap the benefits of the marketing planning analyses described in this book, an information collection/analysis system should be developed within the organization. This could be a formal system designed by the corporation, but for marketing planning, where the focus is the individual product/service level, the system could, in fact, be informally instituted by the brand or product manager. What is more critical, of course, is not whether the system is formalized with forms and manuals or limited to a one-page set of guidelines, but whether the steps recommended are actually followed.

Montgomery and Weinberg (1979) propose the Strategic Intelligence System shown in Figure 7–1. It is a useful example of a planning structure emphasizing the collection and analysis of information about the competitive business environment.

The first parts of the intelligence cycle direct the information collection process and the actual data collection process. In this book, we have attempted to explicitly deal with this issue by (1) describing the major areas of information required (e.g., competitors, customers, and so on), (2) within each major area, being specific about what is the most impor-

FIGURE 7–1
The Strategic Intelligence System

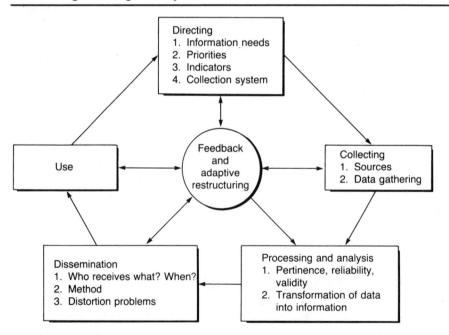

Source: David B. Montgomery and Charles B. Weinberg, "Toward Strategic Intelligence Systems," *Journal of Marketing* 43 (Fall 1979), p. 00.

tant information to collect, and (3) demonstrating where and how such information can be collected.

Clearly, once the information has been gathered, some form of computerized database system can be established. With information collected from informal (e.g., observation, discussion) and printed sources, this implies the somewhat tedious task of inputting the data into the computer. However, by focusing only on key information needs, we have tried to mitigate the pain as much as possible.

It is, however, worth noting that much business data is already available on computerized databases which are available from vendors. Data can be easily downloaded to mini- or microcomputers to facilitate rapid assimilation into the planning system. Some of these databases are listed in Stewart (1984). We present a representative listing in Table 7–1 of what kind of services are available which specialize in data most relevant to marketing planners.

The services listed in Table 7–1 enable marketing managers to quickly and easily access data and subsequently download it to a local computer for analysis. While the number of services available is already large and fast growing, "supermarkets" of service exist. For example, DIALOG Information Services, Inc. (3460 Hillview Avenue, Palo Alto, CA 94304) is a super-database containing ADTRACK, Donnelly Demographics, FIND/SVP Reports, Moody's Corporate News–U.S., and TRADEMARKSCAN of the list in Table 7–1 plus many others. Thus, "one-stop shopping" for market research information is possible. In addition, publications are available to inform database users of current and future trends in the on-line information business. For example, *Online Access* is published bimonthly.

After the data collection phase, the information must be processed and transformed into a meaningful form for analysis. This is an extremely difficult phase because (1) the quantity of information is enormous, and (2) there is usually a range of data types from quantitative (e.g., sales) to qualitative (e.g., what strategy competitor A is employing). Although we sidestep the data management issues here, there are significant difficulties in both the human and information system dimensions of transforming a mass of data into a form usable for analysis.

The subsequent dissemination phase is related to the discussion in Chapter 1 concerning how the planning is done. The major message of past experience is that for planning to be successful, it must be a joint top-down and bottom-up effort. As a result, data dissemination in the

TABLE 7–1
Representative List of Computerized Marketing Databases

Database	Description	Source
ADTRACK	References to print advertisements in over 150 major consumer and business publications	The Kingman Consulting Group, Inc. 1421 Energy Park St. Paul, Minn. 55108
ARBITRON Information on Demand	Data on TV and radio markets including audience psychographics and ratings	Arbitron 1350 Avenue of the Americas New York, N.Y. 10019
Donnelly Demographics	1980 census data and projections	Donnelly Marketing Information Services 1351 Washington Blvd. Stanford, Conn. 06902
FIND/SVP Reports	Directory of market studies	FIND/SVP 500 Fifth Avenue New York, N.Y. 10110
Moody's Corporate News–U.S.	Current information on more than 13,000 publicly held U.S. companies	Moody's Investors Service, Inc. 99 Church St. New York, N.Y. 10007
MRI Business-to-Business	Results of interviews with managers about their purchases of business products	Medimark Research, Inc. 341 Madison Avenue New York, N.Y. 10017
Study of Media	Demographics, psychographics and product usage data of more than 19,000 adults	Simmons Market Research Bureau, Inc. 219 East 42nd Street New York, N.Y. 10017
TRADEMARKSCAN	All active registered and pending trademarks and inactive trademarks back to 1983	Thomson & Thomson 1 Monarch Drive North Quincy, Mass. 02171
VALS/MRI	Marries MRI consumer information on adult media and product usage with the nine VALS lifestyle types developed by the Stanford Research Institute	Mediamark Research, Inc. 341 Madison Ave. New York, N.Y. 10017

marketing planning context involves brand managers, corporate planners, and field salespeople; that is, a combination of line, staff, and field personnel.

Finally, the information collected, processed, and disseminated must be put together in a useful fashion for developing marketing strategy. In the next two sections of this chapter, we discuss both qualitative and quantitative approaches for assimilating the information.

SCENARIO ANALYSIS

Scenario analysis is the construction of hypothetical events based on alternative sequences of causal factors. According to Kahn and Wiener (1967), they address two types of questions: (1) How might a hypothetical situation arise, step by step? and (2) What are the alternative courses of action available to the decision maker(s) to either cope with the hypothetical outcomes or to affect the sequence of events?

The construction and analysis of scenarios has been utilized by policymakers for many years. The technique is closely associated with the late Herman Kahn and the global forecasts produced by the Hudson Institute. However, a series of articles by Wack (1985a, 1985b) in the *Harvard Business Review* demonstrated how Royal Dutch/Shell adapted the approach to corporate planning. In particular, scenario planning is credited with convincing senior management of the eventuality of the 1973 Arab oil embargo and the ultimate shift in market power from buyers to sellers in the worldwide market for oil.

Wack (1985a) describes two stages in scenario planning analysis. The first he refers to as "first-generation" scenarios. These simply combine levels of uncertain outcomes to create a large number of outcome "cells." For example, Figure 7-2 shows a simplified first-generation scenario in the context of financial institutions in 1985. One area of uncertainty for financial institutions was the impact of changes in the tax laws on consumer investment in individual retirement accounts (IRAs). Cell 1 is, of course, the most critical cell as financial institutions have derived a significant amount of capital from IRAs. Cell 4 is the status quo. Cell 3 would be a surprise to IRA marketers and might represent a fundamental shift in investor attitudes toward current consumption. As a result, this combination of events (as well as cell 1) may spur the development of new products. Cell 2 is perhaps the most unlikely outcome. While this analysis does not get at root causes of changes in the planning environment, it

FIGURE 7–2
Simplified First-Generation Scenario

	Customer Behavior	
	Consumers Cut Back IRA Investments	No Behavior Change
Environment:		
Congress restricts investment in IRAs	1	2
Congress does not	3	4

does permit a better understanding of how key factors of the background analysis for marketing planning interact.

The second-generation scenarios are referred to as decision scenarios. These are developed by examining some of the underlying factors which give rise to the uncertainties depicted in the first-generation scenarios. By examining these root causes of uncertainty, marketing planners can better forecast the future business environment and plan appropriate strategies.

Returning to our previous example, we can conjecture some underlying reasons why consumers invest in IRAs and why Congress is considering (continually, it seems) changing the tax code in ways unfavorably to the tax deductibility of IRA investments. Some of these are displayed in Table 7–2. To develop a second-generation scenario, marketing planners would look at the underlying determinants of attitudes and behavior and forecast short-run (for marketing plans) scenarios. One scenario indicates a strong demand for tax-sheltered investments for retirement. Combined with some likely changes in the tax code, financial services firms should be developing new products which can account for possible changes in the tax code but provide retirement benefits. These may very well be services completely different from what we now recognize as IRAs. In addition, these firms should be looking increasingly to find segments of the market to which the new products appeal. For example, people currently covered by an employer's retirement plan may find it difficult to invest in a conventional IRA but may be the best candidates for a "son of" IRA.

The construction of good scenarios requires line management in-

TABLE 7–2
Information Relevant to Second-Generation Scenario

Customer behavior toward IRAs is affected by:
    Increased financial sophistication
    Increasing number of financial products offered
    Increasing disposable income of "baby boomers"
    Increased concern over the long-term viability of the social security system
    Perceived tax benefits
Congressional behavior toward the tax code is affected by:
    Increased perception of the unfairness of the system
    Which party is in power
    Lobbying efforts by special interest groups
    Fiscal health of the economy

volvement since they are the ones facing the uncertainty of the business environment on a day-to-day basis. As noted by Wack (1985a), scenarios help managers deal with uncertainty when (1) the scenarios are based on realistic views of the environment, and (2) they change how managers view the world and challenge conventional assumptions. Real scenarios are obviously much more complex than the one presented above, but out of this complexity comes the disciplined thinking which is a useful by-product of the marketing planning effort.

DECISION-SUPPORT SYSTEMS

For over 15 years, systems have been developed and applied which combine an underlying mathematical structure and managerial judgmental inputs to aid in marketing decision making. These systems can be referred to as *decision support systems* (Blanning, 1984) as they provide easy access to decision models, such as market response models to advertising. The underlying structure can be referred to as a *causal* model as, for example, different levels of advertising spending are presumed to directly affect sales or market share.

There have been many such models described in the marketing literature (see Stewart & Zahorik, 1987, for a review). They are often referred to as *decision calculus* models because of the manager-model interaction required. Montgomery and Weinberg (1973) describe four basic steps in building decision calculus models:

1. Managers are first asked to describe what they feel is the set of factors related to what is being predicted, for example, market share.
2. These factors are then combined in a mathematical model describing the relationship between them and the predictive variable.
3. The model's parameters are estimated, perhaps judgmentally.
4. The managers interact with the model in a "what-if" fashion to see how varying the factors affect the predictor or output variable.

Such decision calculus or support systems have been developed for a wide variety of marketing applications. Such applications include marketing mix variable decisions (Little, 1975), sales force allocation (Lodish, 1971), forecasting of new product sales (e.g., Blackburn & Clancy, 1982; Silk & Urban, 1978), and resource allocation for retailers (Lodish, 1982). Most of these applications have been narrow in scope in that they tend to focus on tactical decisions and incorporate relatively few variables.

An exception is STRATPORT, developed by Larreche and Srinivasan (1981). It is oriented toward helping marketing managers make optimal product portfolio decisions; that is, decide how to allocate cash over different products. It is thus more strategic than other decision support systems which have been developed and is also broader in scope as it has mathematical representations for costs, industry price, and other factors not found in the marketing mix or forecasting models.

There are at least two ways a decision support system could be constructed based on the planning data described in this book. The first way would be to model the system after the type of analysis performed by the profit impact on market strategy (PIMS) project (see Abell & Hammond, 1979, chap. 6). Based on data collected across a large number of firms and industries, the PIMS project utilizes a model that tries to predict line of business return on investment (ROI) as a function of business characteristics, and financial market, and industry data. PIMS thus addresses the following major issues:

1. Why ROI varies between different kinds of businesses.
2. What rate of ROI is normal for a business with a given set of characteristics.
3. How ROI can be affected by a change in corporate strategy.

From a marketing planning perspective, PIMS is too aggregate in that more brand-level implications are needed. However, given data over brands in a market and over several years, it would be possible to relate industry, customer, and competitor characteristics to a brand's profitability and/or market share. Once weights have been found for the characteristics using, say, regression, a manager could try various levels of advertising, demographic groups size, competitor strategy, and so on, and then see how it would impact the brand's performance.

A second approach to building a marketing planning–based decision support system would be to follow the decision calculus style and build a system with several (or many) interrelated response functions. Such a system could look similar to the STRATPORT model discussed earlier but be more comprehensive to include the kinds of data discussed in this book.

LOOKING TO THE FUTURE

We have described in this book a set of steps that are necessary, in our opinion, for marketing managers to follow in order to construct sound marketing plans. These steps are not related to the rate of change of computer or any other technology. Indeed, they would have been as good to follow 20 years ago as today. In addition, it is unlikely that a thorough examination of customers, industry, and competitors will be unnecessary in the year 2000.

The major impediment to marketing planning will not be a lack of information. As Little (1987) notes, in the packaged goods industries, the placement of optical scanning devices in supermarkets has led to a considerable amount of data on market shares and distribution by brand, size, and geographic region. However, "only a few of the intended customers for this data have any idea of how much it is or any idea of what they do with it all if they had it" (Little, 1987, p. 25).

Where technology *can* have an impact, however, is in the processing and use of the large amount of data collected. In particular, it is possible that the rapid increase in artificial intelligence applications to developing expert systems will aid marketing managers in developing strategies from the planning data.

Blanning (1984) defines an expert system for managers (ESM) as

A system that captures specialized knowledge that managers bring to bear on the decision-making tasks they perform, and it uses this knowledge to diagnose potential or actual problems, make recommendations, and offer explanations of its diagnoses and recommendations.

We see at least two potential applications of ESMs to the marketing planning process. First, an ESM could be developed to aid in the forecasting of probable competitor strategies. By building a historical database consisting of various competitor moves under different resource constraints, a system could be built responding to inputs provided by the marketing manager. For example, a manager could input a strategy option and current data on the competitor in responses to queries by the ESM. By using the manager and the competitor, the ESM could help determine the optimal decision rule.

A second potential application of ESMs to marketing planning is to the planning system itself. With high management turnover, there is substantial potential for "memory" loss to occur with respect to the steps to follow in developing a marketing plan. An ESM could be built incorporating the knowledge of prior "experts" who used successful procedures for developing marketing plans. This system would mimic the prior managers' thought processes and thus help to preserve a successful system.

Stewart and Zahorik (1987) are pessimistic about the use of ESMs in marketing because of the purposeful instability of most markets. This makes it difficult to develop an ESM as the decision rule must be adaptive rather than stable. Since there is little opportunity for routinized decision making in marketing, they argue that the value of ESMs is less in marketing applications than in other disciplines, such as medicine, where they have been successfully developed.

This criticism affects mainly the first application discussed here. Random actions by competitors can cause programmed decision rules to be faulty. However, the question is not whether, say, the competitor forecasts are correct 100 percent of the time but whether financial implications of increasing the probabilities of being right justifies the expense of creating the system.

SUMMARY

As is often stated (e.g., Lehmann 1985, chap. 2), unless the odds of making a good decision change as the result of information being collected, then the information has no value. The basic premise of this book is that information about the business environment *has* value to marketing managers in competitive markets. What we have attempted to do in this book is to be explicit about the information and analyses necessary to create value out of the marketing planning activity.

The major analyses we advocate are:

1. *Sales analysis.*   A detailed look at the product's own sales record to analyze sales and market share differences between geographic regions, product sizes, and so on.
2. *Industry attractiveness.*   An assessment of basic industry and environmental factors affecting the product.
3. *Customer analysis.*   An examination of the basic aspects of customer behavior in terms of who they are and why and how they buy.
4. *Competitor analysis.*   Information collected to keep abreast of competitor activities and to enable the manager to predict future competitor product strategies.
5. *Market potential and forecasting.*   Essential, forward-looking activities which help the manager determine appropriate strategic objectives for the product.

Whether better decisions are made as a result of the procedures recommended in this book is difficult to measure since we do not know what would have happened otherwise. However, the mere exercise of collecting and analyzing the data is worthwhile for keeping in touch with rapidly changing markets even if better decisions do not immediately result. Put differently, homework does not always help but even intellectually gifted students or executives are, in general, better off when they do it.

REFERENCES

Abell, Derek F., and John S. Hammond. *Strategic Market Planning.* Englewood Cliffs, N.J.: Prentice-Hall, 1979.

Blackburn, Joseph D., and Kevin J. Clancy. "LITMUS: A New Product Planning Model." In *Marketing Planning Models,* ed. A. A. Zoltners, vol. 18. New York: Elsevier North-Holland, 1982.

Blanning, Robert W. "Management Applications of Expert Systems." *Information and Management* 7 (1984), pp. 311–16.

Kahn, Herman, and Anthony J. Wiener. *The Year 2000.* London: Collier-Macmillan, 1967.

Larreche, Jean-Claude, and V. Srinivasan. "STRATPORT: A Decision Support System for Strategic Planning." *Journal of Marketing* 45 (Fall 1981), pp. 39–52.

Lehmann, Donald R. *Market Research and Analysis.* 2nd ed. Homewood, Ill.: Richard D. Irwin, 1985.

Little, John D. C. "BRANDAID": A Marketing Mix Model. Part I: Structure; Part II: Implementation." *Operations Research* 23 (1975), pp. 628–73.

Little, John D. C. "Information Technology in Marketing." Working Paper # 1860-87, Sloan School of Management, MIT, 1987.

Lodish, Leonard M. "CALLPLAN: An Interactive Salesman's Call Planning System." *Management Science,* vol. 18, (1971), pp. 25–40.

Lodish, Leonard M. "A Marketing Decision Support System for Retailers." *Marketing Science* 1 (Winter 1982), pp. 31–56.

Montgomery, David B., and Charles B. Weinberg. "Modeling Marketing Phenomena: A Managerial Perspective." *Journal of Contemporary Business,* Autumn 1973, pp. 17–43.

Montgomery, David B., and Charles B. Weinberg. "Toward Strategic Intelligence Systems." *Journal of Marketing* 43 (Fall 1979), pp. 41–52.

Silk, Alvin J., and Glen L. Urban. "Pre-Test Evaluation of New Packaged Goods: A Model and Measurement Methodology." *Journal of Marketing Research* 15 (May 1978), pp. 171–91.

Stewart, David W. *Secondary Research.* Beverly Hills, Calif.: Sage Press, 1984.

Stewart, David W., and Anthony J. Zahorik. "Judgmental Data in Marketing Planning Systems." In *Foundations of Expert Systems for Management,* ed. Robert W. Blanning. Koln, West Germany: Verlag-Rheinland, 1987.

Wack, Pierre. "Scenarios: Uncharted Waters Ahead." *Harvard Business Review* 63 (September–October 1985a), pp. 72–89.

Wack, Pierre. "Scenarios: Shooting the Rapids." *Harvard Business Review* 63 (November–December 1985b), pp. 139–50.

INDEX

A

Accuracy, and market forecasting, 117–19
Action programs, and marketing planning, 8–9
ADTRACK database, 161–62
Aggregate market factors, and industry analysis, 40–42
Alternative models of sales as function of population, 144–46
Alternative strategies, and marketing planning, 6
Alternative technological strategies, functional requirements of, 71
Analogous products, and potential estimates, 121
Analysis-based potential estimates, 123–24
A priori segment derivation, 98–99
ARBITRON database, 162
Area potential, and potential estimates, 124–29
Auditing of marketing planning, 9

B

Background assessment, marketing plan, 10–11
Background data, and marketing planning, 7
Bottom-up forecasting, 147
Brand, purchase probability by, 98
Brand franchise, 28
Brand positioning, 66
Brand/product service, assessing value of, 105

Brand switching, 28–29
Budget, and potential estimates, 114
Budget competition, 24–25
Buyers' bargaining power, 45–46

C

Capabilities, assessment of competitors', 70–82
Capital requirements, and new entrants, 44
Compatibility, and product value assessment, 120–21
Competition
  budget, 24–25
  generic, 23, 25
  levels of, 21–26
  product form, 22–23, 25
  rivalry, 24, 47
  similar features, 23
Competitive activity, and customer value, 102
Competitive analysis simplification, 81
Competitive set definition
  competitor determination, methods for, 26–32
  competitor selection, 33–36
  enterprise competition, 35
  levels of competition, 21–26
  overview of, 19–21
Competitor analysis, 11
  competitors' capabilities, assessment of, 70–82
  competitors' current strategies, assessment of, 64–70